THE FINAL ACCOUNTING

ABOUT THE AUTHOR

JOHN MUIGAI MUCAI HAS A PH.D. in Business Administration from the University of Nairobi. He is a Certified Public Accountant of Kenya too. He is an alumnus of the United States International University, where he graduated with an MSc in Management and Organizational Development and a BSc cum laude in Information Systems & Technology. He retired from Coca-Cola East & Central Africa Ltd in 2017 and has since been pursuing various hobbies and entrepreneurial interests.

THE FINAL ACCOUNTING

(VOLUME 1)

A Prelude to Judgment Day

John Mucai

For any further information, contact John Muigai Mucai at the following address:
P.O. Box 2069 - 00606, Nairobi, Kenya. Email:
johnmucai@gmail.com

Cover design by Linda Matama

ISBN 978-9914-40-641-2

*To my wife, Susan, my son Allan, and my
daughter Anne, all of whom are the primary
source of inspiration and encouragement for the
MUCAI Quick Read series.*

"For God shall bring every work into judgment, with every secret thing, whether it be good, or whether it be evil."

ECCLESIASTES 12:14

CONTENTS

FOREWORD

THE FINAL ACCOUNTING IS THE thirteenth book in the MUCAI Quick Read series. The books in the series are for the reader who wishes to indulge in light and educative entertainment. For example, a passenger on a bus, train, cruise ship, or plane heading to a distant destination, a tourist relaxing on a beach on the beautiful coast of Mombasa, or someone just relaxing at home after a long day at work.

The books cover a broad spectrum of topics to titillate the reader's intellect:

- humorous biographical stories
- accounts of captivating historical events
- narratives of extraordinary science
- journeys towards spiritual enlightenment
- intrigues in business
- strategy
- thought-provoking philosophical ideas

The series aims to encourage the reader to think about the world differently and positively. Please visit *mucaiquickread.com* for more information.

PREFACE

AS I START TO WRITE this book, I feel incredibly heavy-hearted because of the atrocious acts that have been deliberately committed by my fellow human beings in different parts of the world. And the wave of brutality of man against man is continuing without any conceivable stop. Four nations that possess the most potent military forces in the globe are currently waging daily indiscriminate bombing campaigns in two of the most impoverished parts of the world, with devastating consequences. The sheer heartlessness is mind-boggling.

It is as if the world has completely lost its direction, and there appears to be no one to steer it back on course. The ones with the power and capacity to change the trajectory seem to be in a state of cowardly paralysis and have decided to look away and, in some instances, are directly abetting the atrocities.

And it gets even more gruesome. Water, energy, food, and medical supplies to one of these impoverished communities that have effectively been under siege for decades have been cut off. The telecommunication links that the people there can use to communicate with the outside world have not been spared.

What is astonishing is that one of the nations committing these heinous crimes has proclaimed publicly that its mission is to drive away or eliminate the impoverished communities, including the entirety of the communities' earthly possessions, so that they can take over the lands of these disadvantaged communities. The aggressor claims they are committing heinous crimes following instructions of their God written in the Old Testament of the Bible more than 2,000 years ago. The absurdity of it all is beyond belief.

The chillingly weird utterances have been supplemented by brazen lies trying to explain away atrocities that have been difficult to hide away from the prying eyes of everyone who has paid even a modicum of interest in the shameful and appalling acts that have found their way on television screens, and other popular socio-media channels.

And as if to add salt to injury, reports coming out of official government communication channels of the Western countries and the mainstream media houses are grotesquely biased and, in many cases, outright misleading.

Debates in parliaments of some Western countries are characteristic of their heartless rhetoric. And even worse, in some houses of parliament, discussions have been permanently stifled by the ubiquitous, yet clandestine, actors who operate in the dark and have unlimited power to muzzle almost anyone who gets in their cross-hairs.

In some quarters, the airwaves have been completely jammed by unspeakable silence.

I feel a mixture of anger, disbelief, and nausea. May the Almighty God have mercy on the helpless people and end their extreme suffering.

While all these Armageddon scenarios have been playing out, humanity has been treated to another ghastly scandal that has desecrated most news channels. A massive network of pedophilia and other forms of sex abuse, allegedly involving some of the wealthiest, most powerful, and most influential individuals in the world, was discovered and continues to rear its ugly head. The abuses appear to have occurred over more than 20 years. It is simply alarming. And yet, only two people have gone to jail for the crimes – one of them committed suicide in highly suspicious circumstances. The evil network would probably never have been discovered were it not for a court case initiated by one of the victims, now a middle-aged woman who is haunted by her past to an unimaginable extent.

It has been alleged that the mastermind of the pedophilia ring had installed sophisticated CCTV cameras in the residences where the abuse of children and minors was taking place. One can, therefore, not help asking the question of whether the footage of the CCTV recordings is part of the explanation for the apparent paralysis we are seeing on the world stage today on the part of some influential leaders in society in the face of unfolding devilish atrocities being committed before our very eyes, every day?

Or could it be all a matter of just primitive human hatred, anger, revenge, racialism, greed, arrogance, conceit, self-aggrandizement, or other abhorrent human traits? Maybe, one day, we will know the answers to these questions. The narrative in this book suggests we will.

Sometimes, I have felt completely powerless and helpless in the face of all these endless absurdities. I have concluded that life without hope is the saddest condition for mankind. How tragic!

Upon reflection a few days ago, it struck me that every human phenomenon that has been unfolding before our eyes is a function of the actions of individuals. Whether the individuals have been acting independently or as a collective, at the end of the day, it boils down to individual action.

In many situations, the collective actions of multiple individuals are what have manifested into the phenomena that continue to shape our global landscape.

This realization opened my mind to the fact that my voice, no matter how low, may contribute to reshaping events towards a better common human future that we can all cherish irrespective of our stations in life.

But what can a single individual like me do to achieve such a grand purpose? On the face of it, it may seem minor and even futile. But the reality is that many good things we enjoy today can be attributed to the proactive actions of an individual who pointed mankind in a new direction in a particular sphere of life. You know some of these individuals.

In this book, I try to accomplish a similar purpose by focusing the world's attention on one simple thing: **personal accountability**. I do this by appealing to people's sensibilities based on their sense of spirituality, irrespective of their religious affiliation or lack thereof.

The truth is that every person, irrespective of their faith or none thereof, has a compass that guides their life. Whether or not they make a meaningful effort to adhere to that compass is beside the point. The critical point is that there is a frame of reference they relate to in their private moments, and that drives their actions.

I would find it hard to believe that there is an individual in this world who simply passes their time from day to day without thinking about their *raison d'etre*.

When one's actions deviate from this frame of reference, it is reasonable to assume that one would, at a minimum, feel some angst and make an effort to moderate one's future behavior. If this was not the case, then the world would be a concoction of untold chaos that could barely have survived to become what it is today.

In this book, I use a metaphor of the "Last Interview" before "Judgment Day" to sensitize every reader about the ultimate accountability they must all face. I aim to prick the consciences of as many individuals as possible in the hope that I can influence someone out there to moderate their behavior or the behavior of other individuals for the collective good of mankind.

The Last Interview is a preliminary stage where everyone will be given a chance to reflect on their deeds before judgment is rendered on Judgment Day." You can think of the Last Interview as a dress rehearsal for Judgment Day.

I have used satire and humor in the belief that this narrative style will attract the most significant readership. Also, satire and humor are uniquely effective ways of communicating a message, no matter how serious, without provoking a negative and counter-productive reaction from the target audience.

It may sound oxymoronic to use satire and humor to tackle such weighty and gruesome subjects as war, genocide, and human rights violations – to mention just a few.

But I take the view that satire and humor have the potency to provide the required amelioration amid all anger, fear, cowardice, egocentricity, and the other drivers of the madness we are witnessing.

If, after reading this book, you will do something, no matter how small, that may help in resolving the current insanity we are witnessing, may God Almighty shower you with blessings in abundance.

The names and accounts of many characters in the book are fictitious. This will be self-evident from the narrative. However, there are instances where I have used the real names and accounts of individuals who are critical actors in the chaos. In most cases, I have used direct quotations of their utterances from publicly available sources.

I have gone to extraordinary lengths to ensure I do not inaccurately describe someone or their actions. If a reader comes across any such inadvertence, I kindly request they bring it to my attention. I undertake to take all humanly possible actions to make a speedy correction.

For example, the histories presented in the chapter on politicians are based on documented historical facts. In some cases, the information has been quoted verbatim from a historical record. All direct quotes are shown in block format using Calibri fonts with the appropriate credit to the source shown as endnotes.

John Mucai

Having said that, recent contemporary events have clearly shown that some histories must be taken with a pinch of salt, as gas-lighting seems to have become the norm in some of what one would have previously assumed to be highly respectable circles where deliberate distortion of facts ought to be anathema. But such is the low level to which society has descended and is indeed the underlying reason for the publication of this book.

ACKNOWLEDGMENTS

The Almighty God has been the shining guiding light throughout my life, even in this book project. I will always remain steadfastly thankful to Him.

This book would not have been possible without the ongoing unshakeable support of my wife, Susan, my son, Allan, and my daughter, Anne. I am deeply grateful to them.

I would also like to thank Rose Muyah and Nzisa Kattambo for reviewing the book and offering valuable feedback.

CHAPTER 1

The Setting

"But if we were more discerning with regard to ourselves, we would not come under such judgment."
—Corinthians 11:31

FIRST THINGS FIRST: ON JUDGMENT DAY, the luxury of remaining silent to avoid self-incrimination will not be available. So, Americans, you can say adios *amigos* to pleading the 5th. Canadians, you will have to come clean as you are. The Charter of Rights and Freedoms will not protect you. You will be on your own. Germans. Forget the *Grundgesetz* guarantees. You will not need them. You will just have to talk and defend yourself *ab initio*. Kenyans, Article 49 of the Constitution will not apply. You will have to account for your actions without any legal crutches.

If you are not an American, Canadian, German, or Kenyan, do not get the false impression that you will have such earthly privileges either. Judgment Day will be a day of full personal accountability. No defense lawyers to plead on your behalf, no earthly laws to seek loopholes through which you can escape. Nothing - just you and yourself. But you will have one final chance to explain yourself: the Final Accounting.

Setting for the Final Accounting

The setting for the final accounting will be simple and very similar to an earthly courtroom.

The Chief Interviewer will sit on an elevated seat at the front of the humongous Interview Room.

Four assistants will sit next to the Chief Interviewer, two to the left and the other two to the right. The First Assistant will maintain a digital record of the proceedings (DRP). The Second Assistant will be responsible for controlling an immensely sophisticated device that will project life histories on a giant Hologram Platform of Life Histories in the middle of the Interview Room (the HPLH), visible to all participants of the proceedings. The life histories will be connected to cables for live streaming across the globe.

The Second Assistant will also be responsible for the Mind Scan System (the MSS), which the panel will use to examine the thought processes of the interviewees at any time in their respective lives.

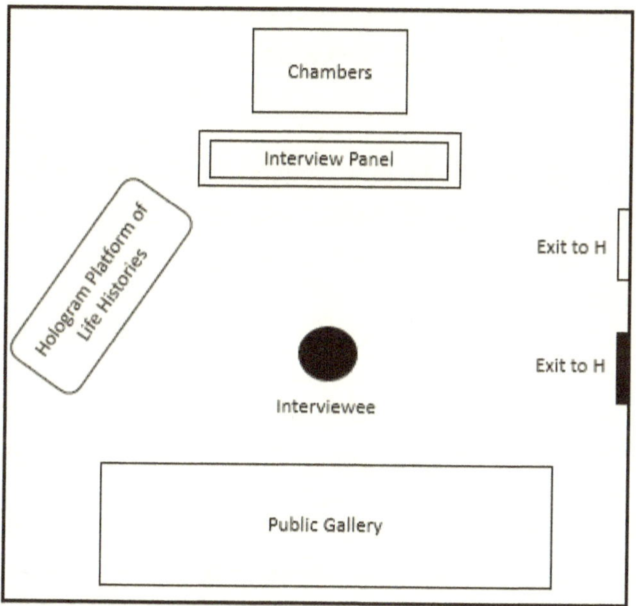

Figure 1: The Interview Room

The Third Assistant will be responsible for documenting invalid excuses in the Grand Book of Lame Excuses (the GBLE). The Fourth Assistant will be the custodian of the Database of Confessions and Forgiveness (BCF).

The interview panel will have access to a remote technical team located in an Equipment Control Booth behind the Interview Room. The technical team will control the DRP, HPLH, MSS, and BCF systems.

There will be a single seat in the center of the room, directly in front of the Chief Interviewer's seat. This seat will be reserved for the Interviewee.

A designated elevated space at the front left-hand side of the Interview Room will serve as an observation deck for angels.

There will be two exit doors from the Interview Room for exclusive use by the interviewees after the interview panel determines their classification. The doors will be marked H and H. Angels will direct the interviewees to the applicable exit door.

This format will likely feel familiar to TV viewers, except for the two unique exit doors. It's a format utilized in numerous countries, particularly in America, where politicians convene in specialized rooms within the Congress premises. These rooms serve as platforms for politicians to interrogate their counterparts in the executive branches of government and other individuals in the private sector. The setting provides a comfortable and sophisticated quasi-judicial environment, all under the watchful gaze of TV cameras. However, in many instances, politicians exploit this setting to showcase their exceptional eloquence, aiming to score political points against their adversaries.

Please note the absence of any provision for any counsel to represent the interviewee. Such representation will be unnecessary. The operating principle will be "everyone for himself."

CHAPTER 2

The Pre-Interview Conference

*"Nothing spoils a good story than the
arrival of an eyewitness."*
—Mark Twain

THE SUCCESS OF ANY IMPORTANT proceedings is a direct function of thorough preparations. All the participants must fully understand the details of the entire process and what will be expected of them. The Final Interview will be no different, which is to be expected, given the status of the interview panel.

Introductory Remarks in Chambers

During the Pre-Interview Conference, the Chief Interviewer will lay out the *modus operandi* of the whole process, which will be something along the following lines:

"Before we begin, I need to clarify the purpose of the upcoming interview process and, even more importantly, what it is not.

"The primary purpose is to allow the interviewees to understand what Judgment Day will entail so that they are not taken by surprise. Our operating principle will be transparency. To this end, the life histories of all interviewees will be laid bare in the Hologram Platform of Life Histories for everyone to see. However, the interview panel will exercise its discretion on whether to show the entire life history of an interviewee or segments of it.

"When the interviews begin, you will gain a first-hand understanding of the importance of this discretionary power. For example, the panel may find certain aspects of an interviewee's life mundane and with no flavor at all. Accordingly, they may decide to skip such segments unless an interviewee requests to have the excluded segment presented as evidence of a particular attribute of their life to which the interviewee would wish to draw to the attention of the interview panel.

Interview Infrastructure

"Two instruments will be of crucial importance. Firstly, a projector (The Hologram Projector or THP in short) that will display an interviewee's life on the Hologram Platform of Life Histories before us.

Paul, in the booth, will do the hologram projection that will allow us to view the entire life of an interviewee. However, an interviewee will have a chance to request a fast forward or a rewind as they consider appropriate. For example, to elucidate a point they believe may not be apparent without the benefit of the context of a particular event in their life history.

"The second instrument will be the Mind Scan System (the MSS in short). The MSS will be similar to the THP except that it will show us the thinking that was going on inside an interviewee's mind during a particular time in their life. This will help clearly indicate an interviewee's motivations for utterances or actions. And, once again, an interviewee will have the benefit of a fast-forward or rewind. Angeline will manage the MSS, also under the guidance of the Second Assistant Interviewer.

What Interviews Will Not Be About

"Let me now turn to the subject of what the interviews will not be about. Firstly, the interviews will not be an opportunity to correct an interviewee's history.

As participants will appreciate, we can rewind the THP or the MSS to clarify an action or a thought that was conceived, but we cannot reverse time. What happened, happened. Full stop.

"Secondly, the interviews are not intended to render any judgment. The day for judgment will come later. The idea of the interviews is to lay out the facts before each interviewee. And, more importantly, to classify the interviewees.

Grouping of Interviewees

"As we speak, all interviewees have been put into homogenous groups and held in the distinct pre-numbered holding rooms they belong to.

"Please note that some individuals may belong to multiple groups due to their unique life histories and thoughts. Great attention has been paid to such individuals to determine the predominant traits in their life histories. Accordingly, they have been put in groups with the highest preponderance of such characteristics.

"I will give you an example. A person may have spent most of their life working as a movie star but joined politics in their retirement days. In this situation, the angels reviewed the careers the interviewees enjoyed most or that enabled them to have the most significant impact on society and grouped them accordingly. In our example, the interviewee would be put in the movie stars' room.

"As you can well imagine, this has been a complex exercise. But the angels have done a splendid job of ensuring that no interviewee feels lonely or short-changed by being in a particular group.

"Of course, there are a few instances where it has proved impossible to determine the preponderance of traits. Individuals who fall into this category have been put in a General Group.

"The rooms in which the interviews are held have been numbered randomly to ensure fairness in the interview process. Interviews will be conducted sequentially, starting with interviewees in Room #1. However, I reserve the discretion to change the sequence for any valid reason that may emerge during the interview process.

"All interviewees will wait in their respective rooms until they are called by one of the angels assigned to their Room. The angels will ensure that all interviewees remain comfortable as they await to be contacted.

Key Outputs: Classification of Interviewees

"What will be the key output from our proceedings in this celestial Interview Room? The answer is simple. It is the classification of interviewees into two essential categories. I will talk about these categories momentarily.

"The classification of each interviewee has already been determined based on the evidence of their respective life histories. However, we must validate the data against what is recorded in the Book of Confessions and Forgiveness (the BCF). Why is this important?

"The angels who have been the custodians of the BCF database have brought to our attention numerous instances where entries have been made in the BCF that have mutated multiple times during an interviewee's lifetime. For example, some entries in the database were created at the minuscule instances of transition when an interviewee was moving from the earthly to the abeyance state. We need to seek clarification as to where the interviewee truly belongs.

"Let me now explain the classifications we will focus on during the interviews. We have the H and H classifications. This is the most critical classification. An interviewee will fall into one of these categories depending upon their performance during the interview.

"I know many of you are already wondering what the difference between these two classifications is. You need not worry about that. The angels in charge of logistics are well-versed in the distinction between these two classifications. After the interviews, they will usher the interviewees to their appropriate rooms (i.e., H or H). The idea here is to ensure speedy delivery of justice during Judgment Day.

The Interview Panel

"Let me transition now to the interview panel. I will be the Chief Interviewer. I will be assisted by four qualified interviewers of the Final Kingdom. The First Assistant Interviewer will focus on actions and thoughts. The Second Assistant Interviewer will focus on deliberate acts of commission. The Third Assistant Interviewer will pay attention to excuses. The Fourth Assistant Interviewer will work closely with the angel in charge of the Book of Confessions and Forgiveness (BCF) to determine entries that require confirmation or erasure.

"At the end of every interview, we will take a brief recess in the chambers to determine an interviewee's classification and the next room they will be dispatched to. In other words, whether it will be H or H to await the final decision on Judgment Day.

The Interview Methodology

"An angel will bring an interviewee to the designated spot at the center of the Interview Room. I will ask the interviewee to give an account of their life. They will have one hour to give the account, but they will be free to continue for as long as they wish with my permission. But, my colleagues on the interview panel can limit the time if the interviewee veers off on a tangent and starts wasting our time.

All the evidence will be available on the HP and the MSS, so interviewees will not need anyone to help them present an account of themselves. That is the beauty of the interview process.

All deliberations in this courtroom will be in the English language. Non-English speakers will have all the necessary interpretation facilities. The language angels will be available to provide any language support the interviewees need.

Concluding Remarks

"Angels, please communicate the pertinent elements of this process to the interviewees under your care.

"May the Almighty God bless these proceedings."

CHAPTER 3

Room 19: Ten-Year-Olds

"Surely I was sinful at birth,
sinful from the time my mother
conceived me.."
— *Psalm 51:5*

THE INTERVIEWS FOR INDIVIDUALS IN Rooms 1 to 19 went quite smoothly. Having had only limited exposure to the world, the interviewees did not have much to account for their brief sojourn on Earth. Most of the individuals were ushered into Room H. There were only a few cases where the interview panel had no choice but to have the individuals ushered into the other room. However, there was a dramatic incident before the last two Room 19 interviews.

A Dramatic Beginning

Just as the Chief Interviewer was about to begin the day's session, the angel in charge of Room 1201 rushed in, panting. The angel had some urgent information they wanted to communicate to the Chief Interviewer.

"What is it, my angel?" the Chief Interviewer inquired.

"My Dear and Most High Majesty, there is a fracas in Room 1201," she said.

"The politicians are agitating that they should be given priority in these proceedings," the angel responded.

"Why is that?" the Chief Interviewer asked.

"They claim that most of them held leadership positions during their sojourn on Earth and that they have the right to be heard before the minions they led. They claim it would be demeaning for them to be so far back in the queue.

"They were extremely unruly and threatened to use all of their powers to cause a revolt in all the rooms if their request is not accepted," the angel replied.

"Who was the ring leader in that fracas," asked the Chief Interviewer.

"The most unruly one is called Adolf. He has a strange mustache and is easily recognizable from the other lot. He says he was a member of the Third Reich and never tolerated any delays. Therefore, he will not accept any delays in this place either.

"Tell Adolf and his colleagues that their request has been denied. Additionally, tell them that their agitation has been duly recorded and will be an important consideration when the interview panel makes its recommendations after the interviews." The Chief Interviewer made this pronouncement affirmatively, sending shock waves in the Interview Room.

"We will not waste any more time. Please bring in the next interviewee from Room 19," the Chief Interviewer said, with his gaze directed at the elevated angels gallery.

Enter Justin Ogunlade

Justin Ogunlade was duly ushered into the Room. He was dressed in children's jeans and a matching navy blue shirt. He also wore a sophisticated-looking T-shirt his parents had bought him from one of the reputable online stores in Lagos, Nigeria.

"Please introduce yourself to the Interview Panel," the First Assistant Interviewer asked.

"My name is Justin Ogunlade. I hail from Owode, which is in the Ogun State of Nigeria. I am ten years old and attended the Abraham Oliyide Nursery and Primary School before I suddenly found myself here. I have two brothers and four sisters. My father is a carpenter and has a workshop at Batolu, o!" Justin said.

"My mother just stays at home, doing nothing, o!" added Justin.

The interviewers almost laughed, but protocol dictated they refrain from showing any emotions during such proceedings.

"Good. We are glad for your brief and clear introduction of yourself," the First Assistant Interviewer said.

"Now, Justin. I am sure the angel in charge of your Room has already explained why you are here today. So, I will go straight to the point as we have many other individuals to interview.

"So, without much further ado, please give us an account of your life on Earth. From time to time, during your presentation, we may play a video of certain segments of your life to refresh your memory. We may also activate the mind-reading system to get additional insights that will help us fully understand the motivations of your actions and non-actions. Is that clear?" the Chief Interviewer asked.

"Yes, Sir," Justin responded.

"OK! You may proceed," The Chief Interviewer said.

"Sir, I am not sure where to start, but I will try my best," Justin said.

"Don't worry. We will help you," the Chief Interviewer said.

"Paul, please run the THP from age 8," the Chief Interviewer said.

When Justin saw his life playing on the giant Hologram Platform of Life Histories in technicolor, he was utterly dumbfounded. He saw how loudly he cried when, one day, his mother returned from shopping and did not have the lollipops Justin had asked her to buy.

He saw how, on a different occasion, he had teased his sister Josephine in front of her classmates simply because she had become number 1 in her end-of-term exams. Justin was number 20 out of 30 in his class and was jealous of his sister.

Justin saw how his parents were always happy when he woke up early on a Sunday morning to attend Sunday School, especially when he volunteered to say a Bible verse in front of the church congregation.

"The tapes have shown everything about me. I have nothing to add," Justin said.

"However, there is only one thing I would like to say. When I called my sister "donkey," I did not mean it. I was just joking," Justin said.

"Is that so? Well, let us examine what you really meant. Angeline, please roll the MSS, starting two minutes from the point where Justin uttered the word donkey," the Chief Interviewer said.

I will say something nasty to her so that she can feel hurt as much as possible. She is a good-for-nothing sister. I wish she had not been born into this household.

"So, what do you have to say about those thoughts?" the Chief Interviewer asked Justin.

"I am so sorry, Sir! I had forgotten about that. Please forgive me," Justin said.

"Thank you! Now we have a good idea about you, Justin. The interview panel will now retire briefly in the chambers to review your case and determine the next step.

While the interviewers were reviewing the interviewee's performance, the Chief Interviewer asked Judith, the custodian of the BCF database, to check the instances when Justin had sincerely confessed to his transgressions and asked for forgiveness.

"We can see only one instance when he had done that, My Dear and Most High Majesty. That was when he was 9 years and 5 months old. He was engaged in a fight with one of his classmates, Oleshegun, related to the theft of Oleshegun's pencil. Oleshegun had received intelligence from another child, clearly pointing to Justin as the culprit.

"Oleshegun had wasted no time. He was a bigger boy than Justin. He had accosted Justin during the class break. During the ensuing fight, he had caught Justin in a stranglehold and demanded a confession and apology. Justin had no choice but to confess to the theft. He also sought forgiveness and promised to return the pencil immediately after break time," Angeline said.

"My fellow interviewers, what do you think of this case?" The Chief Interviewer asked.

"His classification is obvious. Justin needs to be ushered to Room H," said the First Assistant Interviewer. All the other interviewers nodded in agreement.

The interview panel returned to the Interview Room. The Chief Interviewer asked Justin to stand up.

"We have reviewed your case closely. Given the life you led on Earth, your actions and motivations for those actions, and the practical steps you took to steer your life in different directions, we have concluded that you belong to the classification H. The angels present will guide you to Room H to await your final judgment," the Chief Interviewer said.

"Sir! Will I get another chance to present a better account of my life?"

"No."

Three angels then ushered Justin to Room H.

"Please usher in the next interviewee," the Chief Interviewer said.

Enter Honest Mangwanani

Honest Mangwanani was duly ushered into the Room. He wore a simple, brownish, Kaunda-like suit with matching shoes. He wore a big smile on his face, projecting tremendous personal confidence.

"Why are you smiling?" the Second Assistant Interviewer asked.

"I am just feeling good for being here, although it was rather sudden, I must admit."

"Please introduce yourself to the interview panel," the Second Assistant Interviewer said.

"Yes. My name is Honest Mangwanani. I was born in Zimbabwe at a place called Murambinda. My parents passed away when I was 6. I was raised by my uncle, Mr. Goodluck Moyo. I was a student at Murambinda B Primary School before I suddenly came here," said Honest.

"Thank you for introducing yourself," the Second Assistant Interviewer responded.

"Now, Honest. The angel in charge of your Room must have already explained the purpose of our session today, right?" the Second Assistant Interviewer asked.

"Yes, Sir," Honest responded.

"Good. May I ask you to please give us an account of your life on Earth. From time to time, during your presentation, we may play a video of certain segments of your life to refresh your memory. We may also activate the mind-reading system to get additional insights that will help us fully understand the motivations of your actions and non-actions. Is that clear?" the Chief Interviewer asked.

"Yes," Honest replied.

"Please proceed," the Chief Interviewer said.

"How do I give an account of my life, Sir? Can I just start anywhere?" Honest asked.

"Feel free to start anywhere. Think about the good or not-so-good things you did on Earth before you came here," the Second Assistant Interviewer said.

"OK! Firstly, I was always a very humble person. I respected my uncle and my aunt very much. I did everything they asked me to do.

"I was always punctual at school, listened attentively to all my teachers, and completed my homework on time. Because of my good behavior, I was appointed a school prefect in class 6. When I joined Class 7, I was appointed head boy of Murambinda B Primary School.

"I was a founding member of the school's debating club and participated in three inter-school debate competitions. My school was the overall winner in all three debating competitions. However, one day, at around 08:00 pm, as we were returning from Harare, where we had just won the third debating competition, something suddenly happened. All I can remember is a loud bang, "ka-boom," followed by darkness. The next thing I experienced was being comfortably seated in Room 19 with some debating club colleagues.

"That is all I can say for now," Honest said.

"Thank you very much, Honest," said the Chief Interviewer.

"We greatly appreciate your honesty," said the Second Assistant Interviewer.

"Paul, please run the THP on the day of the third debating club competition. I am curious to see how Honest performed," the Chief Interviewer said.

The THP projection showed Honest debating eloquently and with tremendous zeal. He opposed the motion that:

"All parents should be compelled to give their children pocket money of 10,000 Zimbabwe Dollars at the beginning of every school term."

Honest had argued strongly against the motion, claiming that many school children were from poor families and the parents could not afford to give their children any pocket money, let alone 10,000 Zimbabwe Dollars. He also impressed the panel of interviewers by pointing out the corrosive effects of money on the lives of youngsters in school; for example, encouraging students to eat too many sweets and chocolate bars, which were detrimental to the students' dental hygiene. He made many other strong arguments.

The hologram display triggered fond memories for Honest. He could not believe it was him doing so well on the podium at Gateway Primary School in Harare. How nice!

"Let us have a quick look at the MSS for the same period," the Second Assistant Interviewer said.

Angeline rolled the MSS tape as requested. Below is a snapshot of the MSS.

It pains me to oppose this motion, knowing fully well how bad I felt when Uncle Goodluck refused to give me even as little as 1,000 Zimbabwe Dollars to come here to participate in this crazy debate today.

Life is cruel because I now have to stand up here and vehemently argue in favor of something I do not believe in.
If our team loses, is there a chance that parents will somehow get to know about it and always make sure to budget for enough pocket money for their children?

I am sure even poor parents can find some money to give their children, even if it is not the whole 10,000 Zimbabwe Dollars.
If I help my team to successfully oppose this motion, all the primary school children in Harare and Mangwanani will hate me.

But, no. I must impress all these beautiful girls in the auditorium that I am a debating expert. Not only that. I can speak English better than any Englishman they will ever come across in Zimbabwe. That is what matters most to me right now.

Honest was astounded but waited for the tape to finish running so that he could explain himself to the interview panel.

"So, what do you have to say about those thoughts, Honest?" the Chief Interviewer asked Honest.

"I am so sorry, Sir! My thoughts were not consistent with what I was saying. But it was just a debate, and I did not think my personal beliefs mattered. I thought it was essential to help my team win the debate, " Justin said.

"Thank you! Now we have an excellent idea about you. The interview panel will now retire in the chambers briefly to review your case and determine the next step," the Chief Interviewer said.

As was customary when the interviewers reviewed the interviewee's performance, Judith perused the BCF database to check the instances when the interviewee sincerely confessed to his transgressions and asked for forgiveness.

"What have you discerned from the BCF database?" the Chief Interviewer asked Judith.

"Well, My Dear and Most High Majesty, I have confirmed that Honest said a short prayer every night before going to bed. It was a standard prayer in which he confessed all his sins and asked for forgiveness.

"The only anomaly I see is that the school bus overturned about 10 kilometers from his home. So, by the time of his exit from Earth, he had not had a chance to confess and seek forgiveness for his inappropriate thoughts during the debate in Harare."

"My fellow interviewers, what do you think of this case?" The Chief Interviewer asked.

"Honest was an honest young man with a promising career ahead of him. He had not been ensnared by worldly evils, but he was sliding on a slippery slope going by some of his thoughts during the debate in Harare. But, on balance, I would recommend an H classification," said the Second Assistant Interviewer.

"Me too," said the First Assistant Interviewer.

"Me too," stated the Third Assistant Interviewer.

"I concur," said the Fourth Assistant Interviewer.

The interview panel returned to the Interview Room. The Chief Interviewer asked Honest to stand up.

"We have reviewed your case closely. Given the life you led on Earth, your actions and motivations for those actions, and the practical steps you took to steer your life in different directions, we have concluded that you belong to the classification H. The angels present will guide you to Room H to await your final judgment," the Chief Interviewer said.

"Thank you," Honest replied.

Three angels then ushered Justin to Room H.

"We will take a recess until tomorrow when we shall hear from the next batch of interviewees," the Chief Interviewer said.

CHAPTER 4

Room 420: Teenagers

*"Teenagers: the only people who can
sleep until noon and still be tired."*
— Bill Gates

INTERVIEWS OF TEENAGERS WERE VARIED and complicated. Each day was a roller coaster of intriguing narratives that exhausted the interview panel. Midway through the interviews, the panel decided to take a two-day break to recuperate. When the panel resumed duty, they were energic. They were able to cover interviews of Jane Costa and Muzaffar Kanranjit in record time.

Enter Jane Costa

The angels ushered Jane Costa into the Interview Room. She was about 4 feet tall and wore a knee-length pink dress that seemed to magnify her curvy shape a thousand-fold. One could tell from a distance that she was truly in her prime as a teenager and had a lot to say about her life.

"Welcome to the Interview Room, Jane," the Third Assistant Interviewer said.

"Thank you," Jane responded.

"Please introduce yourself to the interview panel," the Second Assistant Interviewer asked.

"I am Jane Costa from Atlanta, Georgia, in the US," Jane said.

"Continue!" the Third Assistant Interviewer said.

"That's it. There is not much more to say," Jane responded.

"Well! Then, we can proceed to the next stage. Please give us an account of your life on Earth. From time to time, during your presentation, we may play a video of certain segments of your life to refresh your memory. We may also activate the mind-reading system to get additional insights that will help us fully understand the motivations of your actions and non-actions. Is that clear?" the Chief Interviewer asked.

"I am just happy to be here. I've done lots of good stuff in my life. There is really not much I can say about any bad things.

"Oh! Gosh! I almost forgot. There was this time when Josh, my boyfriend, left me for another girl. It was the most devastating time of my life. Josh befriended my best friend, Anita. I could not stand it. I cried a lot when I remembered this cruelty. But I knew that one day, Josh would pay a hefty price for it. What goes around, comes around, " Jane said.

"Please continue," the Third Assistant Interviewer said.

"I wish there was more I could say. But frankly, the rest of it is so boring you will not want to hear it," Jane responded.

"Paul, please roll the THP. You can start from age 13," the Chief Interviewer said.

Jane was astounded by what she saw on the giant Hologram Platform of Life Histories. She saw how she had spent her early teen years paying little attention to school. Surprisingly, Jane was bright and maintained average grades in all subjects. She saw how demanding she was to her parents. She never wanted to miss any party organized by her friends. Her friends considered her a party animal.

Jane occasionally got into trouble with her parents for returning home late at night. But in all instances, her parents were relieved that she returned home completely sober. In their minds, she was just acting her age and would ultimately change as she matured.

But things started changing when she was 18. Her boyfriend, Josh, started becoming elusive. He seemed to have started becoming busy during weekends and had little time to spend in Jane's company.

Then, to her utter dismay, Jane discovered that Josh had entered into a relationship with one of Jane's best friends, Anita. It was a devastating finding that caused Jane tremendous heartache. She became depressed and constantly brooded about how life had conspired against her. It was as if everything in her life had centered around Josh and suddenly came to a halt when Josh evaporated from her orbit.

She could hardly sleep at night. After a while, she started taking sleeping pills. Unfortunately, one day, she took an overdose and was unable to awaken. This event sent shockwaves within her immediate family, circle of friends, neighborhood, school, and even the city of Atlanta.

Her passing was a significant blow to her parents. They had not seen it coming. Jane had not said anything to them about her breakup with Josh. She had kept everything secret. The details only emerged when the police interviewed her closest friends after the incident.

Jane cried as she watched how she carelessly brought her youthful life to an abrupt end. For once, she saw how cruel and selfish she had been to the people who loved her dearly. Jane realized that her mind was preoccupied almost solely with her relationship with Josh. She was blind to the other deep and loving relationships with her siblings, her parents, her relatives, a multitude of friends, and many other acquaintances, all of whom were deeply hurt by the enormous void she had left in their lives.

"Paul, you can halt it there. I think we have seen enough for now," the Chief Interviewer said.

"I believe your memory is now well refreshed. Do you wish to tell us anything more about your life?" the Third Assistant Interviewer asked Jane.

"No," Jane said, sobbing.

"Thank you, Jane! We know it was not easy for you, especially the last few chapters of your life on Earth. The interview panel will now retire briefly in the chambers to review your case. We will be back in a few minutes," the Chief Interviewer said.

"Judith, does the BCF database contain any insights that may help us make our decision on this candidate?" the Chief Interviewer inquired as the interview panel sat to review Jane's case.

"Everything is pretty much the same as for most of the teenagers we have interviewed, except those whose parents embraced religion in one form or another. In other words, her BCF record is virtually blank," Judith said.

"The panel may be interested in reviewing two portions of the MSS that I thought are quite insightful, especially in the context of what happened in the last few days of the candidate's life," Angeline said.

"Please proceed, Angeline. We would be much obliged," the Chief Interviewer said.

Angeline played two segments of the MSS. The first clip related to Jane's thoughts while in church. Her friend, Anita, was four rows in front of her.

The sermon was in progress, but Jane was not paying attention. She was engrossed in other un-churchly matters.

What is it that Josh saw in that girl? Look at her hair. It looks terrible. I hate the ponytail. I would love to use it to strangle her at this very moment. But there are so many people here who would restrain me. Which means it would become double jeopardy for me. But perhaps I can get somebody to do the job. Ah! What an excellent idea! I must explore it seriously after the service.

The second segment was on her last visit to the pharmacy before her exit from Earth.

I will buy a lethal drug that I can surreptitiously put in her food. But this will be a challenge because we hardly meet nowadays.

But wait! I already have a solution. Silly me! I can hire somebody to do it. But no. Where will I get such a person?

This is becoming too much for me. I would rather take an overdose of the pills and end my misery once and for all.

"Thank you, Angeline. That will do," the Chief Interviewer said.

"I am wondering whether we should present these thought processes to Jane before we pronounce our decision?" the Third Assistant Interviewer asked.

"No harm in doing so," the Chief Interviewer said.

"It is essential that she fully understands the basis of our decision. Remember that the fundamental operating principle for these interviews is transparency.

"However, having said that, we need to be careful not to compromise our procedures. Therefore, I suggest we decide now since we have all the necessary information. I doubt Jane will tell us anything that will influence our determination of her case," the Chief Interviewer added.

All members of the interview panel agreed.

After a brief discussion, the panel made a decision.

The interview panel returned to the Interview Room.

"We have reviewed your case closely," the Chief Interviewer said.

"But before we tell you what we have concluded, we would like to present two important segments of your thought processes that we are sure you will recall vividly. Angeline, please roll the MSS," the Chief Interviewer said.

Janet stopped sobbing. Her mannerisms changed entirely as she keenly paid attention to the MSS.

"Sir! That was a tough time for me. I could not control my thoughts. And as you know, I did not take any action to harm Anita despite my evil thoughts. It all remained in my mind. I am really sorry for entertaining such thoughts.

"On the final day on Earth, I was acting out of an unbearable heartache. It was too much for me. But I am sorry, especially for causing so much distress to many people who were close to me," Jane said.

"Thank you for letting us know," the Chief Interviewer said.

"We have deliberated about your case. Given the life you led on Earth, your actions and motivations for those actions, and the practical steps you took to steer your life in different directions, we have unanimously concluded that you belong to the classification H. The angels present will guide you to Room H to await your final judgment," the Chief Interviewer said.

"Thank you," Jane replied.

Three angels escorted Jane to Room H while other angels fetched Muzaffar Karanjit.

Trouble Brewing in Room 1201

As the interview panel waited for Muzaffar to be brought into the Room, an angel from Room 1201 requested permission to address the interview panel.

"You may proceed," the Chief Interviewer said.

"My Dear and Most High Majesty, I wish to report that big trouble is brewing in Room 1201. A few days ago, the gentleman with a mustache started agitating for relocation to the Room for Artists.

He said that it was a well-known fact that he had practiced art in his early days in Austria and that all angels ought to know that that was where his heart really was. Further, he had become a politician almost by accident.

"We declined his request. We advised him that he would have ample opportunity to talk about his earthly desires and proclivities when his turn for the interview arrived.

"But, My Dear and Most High Majesty, it does not end there. Three days ago, after realizing that we could not budge, he started radicalizing some of his Roommates. He said that Room 1201 was intended exclusively for tall people who have blonde hair. Interestingly enough, he is short and does not have blonde hair. Shortly after that, he and a few of his followers started going around Room 1201, insulting the short people and all those without blonde hair, accusing them that they were solely responsible for politicians being so far behind in the interview queue.

"Initially, we thought things would eventually calm down, especially considering the apparent ridiculousness of the propaganda the gentleman and his followers were spreading in Room 1201. But we were astonished as to the speed at which his misinformation was gaining traction.

"Indeed, things started getting downright dangerous when the gentleman and his followers got physical and started pushing the short people and all those without blonde hair to one side of Room 1201. These actions created a fracas in the whole of Room 1201 because the majority of people there did not fit the desired criteria specified by the gentleman with a mustache and his followers.

"But there are several individuals who acquiesced to the machinations of the mustached man. We find it quite strange. It is a phenomenon that the distinguished and most honorable interview panel may wish to explore at the appropriate time using the advanced tools of interviewing at your disposal.

"My Dear and Most High Majesty, in conclusion, we are requesting your guidance on the actions we should take to manage this delicate situation before it gets out of hand," the angel said.

"Thank you for bringing this matter to our attention," the Chief Interviewer said.

The Chief Interviewer then asked Paul and Angeline to run the condensed versions of the THP and MSS for the gentleman with a mustache from early childhood to the end of his days on Earth.

"Thank you, Paul," the Chief Interviewer said after watching and listening to the recordings.

The panel was shocked by the enormous pain and suffering the mustache man caused mankind during his tenure on Earth. The panel determined the gentleman's classification there and then. However, they resolved to continue with the interview schedule as planned. They would deal with the gentleman's case when his turn for interview came.

"Here is what I want you to do," the Chief Interviewer said, addressing the Room 1201 angel.

"Firstly, please inform the gentleman that the interview panel has noted his unbecoming conduct with great concern and is losing its patience.

"Secondly, please ask the architects to immediately create a solitary confinement section in Room 1201 for exclusive use by the gentleman and his followers.

"Finally, please let it be known by him and his followers that the interview panel will not make any changes to the interview queue or any other aspects of the process simply to please him and his cronies. They will have to wait for their turn just like anyone else in Room 1201," the Chief Interviewer said.

"Thank you, My Dear and Most High Majesty. It shall be done," the angel said.

"The interview panel will take a short break before seeing the next interviewee," the Chief Interviewer said. The break was expected, given the exasperation of watching the life history of the gentleman with a mustache.

Enter Muzaffar Karanjit

The angels brought the next teenage interviewee into the Interview Room. He was adorned in a light blue kurta pajama suit with matching shoes. The type of menswear worn during wedding ceremonies by people of northern Indian origin.

"Please introduce yourself to the interview panel," The First Assistant Interviewer said.

"My name is Muzaffar Karanjit. I was born in Lucknow, which is in Uttar Pradesh State, in the northern part of India. My home was about 320 kilometers from the world-famous Taj Mahal temple. I was the last born in a family of eight children. At the time I left Earth, both my father and mother worked for the state government," Muzaffar said.

"Thank you," the Fourth Assistant Interviewer responded.

"The angels in charge of your Room must have already explained to you in detail why you are here today, right?" The Fourth Assistant Interviewer continued.

"Yes, Sir," Muzaffar responded.

"Well then. Please give us an account of your life on Earth. Please note that from time to time, during your presentation, we may play a video of certain segments of your life. We may also activate the mind-reading system to get additional insights into the motivations of your actions and non-actions. Is that clear?" the Chief Interviewer asked.

"Yes, Sir," Muzaffar responded.

"OK! Please proceed," The Chief Interviewer said.

"I went to school at Muftiganj Boys and Girls High School, at Lucknow in Uttar Pradesh. I spent all my school life there, from lower primary through upper primary, high school, until higher secondary.

"My school performance was always good. I was always among the top 10 students, except in my first term in higher secondary school when I fell seriously ill.

"Mathematics and physics were my favorite subjects. I excelled in these two subjects. This was important because I was keen to study engineering at the Indian Institute of Technology in Madras, following the footsteps of my eldest brother, Kumar Jalota, who studied there and eventually went to the US to work for a large multinational company.

"During many school holidays, I visited my grandparents at Allahabad. I used to help them till the land and harvest mangos," Muzaffar said.

"Thank you," said the Fourth Assistant Interviewer.

"Paul, please run the snapshot version of the THP," The Chief Interviewer said

Muzaffar was astounded to see his entire life displayed in the Hologram Platform of Life Histories. Watching some parts of his life he had deliberately left out when giving his life's account was embarrassing. But he hoped the interviewers would understand the situation.

"Paul, please rewind and stop at the date of the first term of high school. Thank you. Muzaffar, can you tell us what is happening there?" the Fourth Assistant Interviewer asked.

"Yes, Sir," Muzaffar started.

"The car from the village in Allahabad had broken down about five kilometers from my home. The mechanic arrived more than five hours later. By the time I arrived home, I felt very sleepy and did not have enough energy to do my homework. That is why I decided to go to Balwant's house and requested that I copy his homework. I promised to help him if he encountered similar problems," Muzaffar said.

"Angeline, please roll the MSS for the same period," the Fourth Assistant Interviewer said.

I am feeling so tired. I know I can finish the homework if I try hard enough. But I know Balwant must have completed his homework. I will convince him to let me copy his work so that I can go to bed early.

"Paul, please rewind the THP for the end-of-term exams," the Fourth Assistant Interviewer said.

Muzaffar could be seen looking at a small piece of paper on his lap and occasionally at the palm of his hands.

"Please zoom in so that we can see clearly what was going on there," the Fourth Assistant Interviewer said.

"That looks like the projectile motion formula. I can also see the energy density formula. These are written on Muzaffar's left palm.

"The item on his palm is some text. It says:

When the body absorbs heat, its temperature increases. When it discharges or loses heat, its temperature falls. The heat capacity is the heat needed to raise the temperature of an object by a calculation of one degree. It can also be calculated as a ratio of the amount of heat energy given to the object for the resulting increase in the temperature. The expression for the heat capacity is $c = \Delta Q / \Delta T$.

"Was this one of those exams where you were top in the physics exam," the Fourth Assistant Interviewer asked.

"Yes, Sir," Muzaffar said hesitatingly.

"But I can explain, Sir. You see if I did not pass the physics exam that term, my chances of joining IIT would have become quite slim. But now I can see I did the wrong thing. I am so so sorry."

"Thank you. The interview panel will now retire briefly in the chambers to review your case. We will be back in a few minutes," the Chief Interviewer said.

"Judith, what does the BCF show?" the Chief Interviewer inquired as the interview panel sat to consider Muzaffar's case.

"It is blank," replied Judith.

"Colleagues, what do you think of this case?" the Chief Interviewer asked.

"When I compare him with the teenagers we have interviewed so far, his character traits are moderate. I would recommend we send him to Room H," said the Fourth Assistant Interviewer. All the other interviewers agreed.

The interview panel returned to the Interview Room. The Chief Interviewer asked Muzaffar to stand up.

"We have reviewed your case closely. Given the life you led on Earth, your actions and motivations for those actions, and the practical steps you took to steer your life in different directions, we have concluded that you belong to the classification H. The angels present will guide you to Room H to await your final judgment," the Chief Interviewer said.

"I thank you," said Muzaffar

Three angels then ushered Justin to Room H.

"We will resume in a week when all of us are fully re-energized and ready to go. Angels, please continue monitoring activities in Room 1201 to ensure things do not get out of control," said the Chief Interviewer.

CHAPTER 5

Interlude

*"The common man is not common –
he is just waiting for his superhero
moment to come, preferably with a
side of pizza."*
— *Stan Lee*

THE PREVIOUS INTERVIEWS OF CHILDREN and teenagers had gone relatively smoothly, albeit with occasional surprises. The next phase of interviews was expected to be challenging. This was well-articulated in the Chief Interviewer's opening statement.

Statement by the Chief Interviewer

"Colleagues. Thank you for your diligence during the first stage of the interviewing process.

I know it may have been tedious at times because of the age and inexperience of the majority of the interviewees. But, no doubt, it has given us the momentum to proceed to the next stage, which will be more challenging.

"In light of the complexity of some of the life histories we will be dealing with, we will need to tweak the process a little. Also, some individuals we will interview are highly opinionated, talkative, and aggressive. This will add a new dimension of complexity to the interviews.

"We will endeavor to stick to the original interview design for the sake of fairness. But we are the gatekeepers between Earth and the afterworld and, therefore, have the discretion to make any changes that would help us achieve our objectives. I welcome your ideas as we go along.

CHAPTER 6

Room 637: Architects

INTERVIEWS OF ARCHITECTS WERE SIGNIFICANT, not only for the nature of the content the interview panel expected to cover but also because they formed a virtual bridge between simplicity manifested in the previous stage of interviews and the impending complexity. Before starting the interviews, the Chief Interviewer asked Paul to run a snapshot of the Earth's built-up environment in 2023 so the panel could get a good sense of what they would be dealing with.

Paul made his presentation systematically, starting from the architecture in the jungles of the Amazon, moving to the villages in the Himalayas, then the favelas in South American countries, to the sub-urban areas of Europe, then the suburbs of Canada, then the urban jungles of Japan, to the high-end suburbs of Barbados, all the way to the sophisticated castles of Europe. At the end of the presentation, the Chief Interviewer stated that the architectural structures were a good indicator of the intellectual capacity of the architects who conceived the structures and the income levels of the people who lived there.

Enter Washington McGeorge Odhiambo

The angels ushered Washington McGeorge Odhiambo into the Interview Room. He was a be-spectacled medium-built gentleman who could easily be mistaken for a medical doctor. He adorned a dark suit, a neat blue shirt, a bow tie, and shiny black shoes. He was clearly a man of class. If he was on Earth, there was no question he would also be carrying car keys for a posh limousine parked outside the Interview Room. But then, he had left that world. He was on a different journey to a destination that the interviewers would shortly determine. He would not need a limousine to travel there.

"Welcome to the Interview Room, Washington," the Chief Interviewer said.

"Thank you. I am obliged," Washington responded.

"Please introduce yourself to the interview panel," the First Assistant Interviewer asked.

"My names are Washington McGeorge Odhiambo. I hail from Kasipul, Bondo, Kenya. That is my ancestral home, but I lived in a house in the suburb of Lavington, in the city of Nairobi, before my life on Earth came to a sudden and unexpected termination. Hence, my presence here today.

"I was a renowned architect in the government of Kenya for no less than 36 years. I met Damaris Gathoni on my first day at the University of Nairobi School of Architecture and Design. I immediately fell in love with her. Our betrothal coincided with our first anniversary after graduating with similar degrees in architecture five years later. However, her focus area was landscaping, while I specialized in urban built environments.

"We sired two beautiful children, Alex and Dorothy, both of whom followed in our footsteps and joined the University of Nairobi to study mechanical engineering and medicine, respectively. That means that upon their graduation, the Odhiambo clan would have no less than eight degree-holders, most of them in respected professions, to boot. And we thank God for that.

"I am a practicing Catholic," Washington said as he concluded his introduction.

"Very impressive introduction," the First Assistant Interviewer whispered to the Second Assistant Interviewer.

"Thank you, Washington, for the good introduction," said the First Assistant Interviewer.

"The angels in charge of your Room must have already explained to you in detail why you are here today, right?" The First Assistant Interviewer asked.

"Yes. That is right, " Washington replied.

"Good, and thanks for your affirmation. Please give us an account of your life on Earth. Please note that from time to time, during your presentation, we may play a video of certain segments of your life. We may also activate the mind-reading system to get additional insights into the motivations of your actions and non-actions. So, let's get started." the Chief Interviewer said.

"Thank you for giving me this opportunity to present my life account to the distinguished panel. I greatly appreciate it," Washington said.

"I will start by giving you a brief pre-amble of my life. I will then delve into some details of my life as a prominent government architect, touching on my immense contributions to the architectural profession and to the people of Kenya in general. In the process, I will clearly demonstrate how the architectural profession stands in juxtaposition between abstruse human desires and actual human resource endowments. This will be a good segway to my concluding remarks. You may ask clarifying questions as we go along or wait until the end to ask all the questions. The choice is yours," Washington said.

"Thank you, Washington. We will be patient and attentive listeners. We will ask our questions at the end of your presentation," the Chief Interviewer said, almost in jest.

"Thank you, too.

"Giving an account of self is an interesting yet complex undertaking. But my career as an architect taught me never to shy away from any challenge. As an architect, it is beholden upon oneself to stretch the imagination and create structures purely from nothingness. Occasionally, one is called upon to almost do some mind-reading as a client plunges into a sea of vagueness, thoroughly unable to accurately communicate to the architect their requirements. This phenomenon was particularly acute in the lower cadres of society, where many clients demanded Ferraris at the price of a Mini.

"I do not profess to be a mind-reader, but those in this craft can vindicate my assertion that ten percent of what we do is not short of an excruciating exercise in telekinetics. It is amazing. But believe you me, that has been the state of the architectural profession for millennia. In other words, an architect doubles up in psychoanalysis and draftsmanship. So, when you see an architect deep in thought in front of his or her canvas, just remember that he or she may be engaged in mental gymnastics as they try to figure out precisely what the client wants and how to actualize it on paper.

"Let me now turn to my life history as a civil servant, working as an architect in the Ministry of Works in Kenya. My tenure there was transformative. My dad always cautioned me about over-zealousness when talking about my accomplishments.

"But going by what the angel in charge of Room 637 told us, this session is different, and I should be candid about everything I did while on Earth to be worthy of the gift of life while I was there. So, I seek your indulgence in advance if you find my exposition a little overboard.

"Firstly, the Architects' Association of Kenya would not have reached where it was by the time of my Earth's exit were it not for my immense contributions during the formative years of the association. I single-handedly developed more than fifteen memoranda on various legislative changes that members of the association had been clamoring for.

"Also, when I joined the government, I convinced the then-permanent secretary for urban planning and development to introduce a low-cost housing program to benefit the low-income members of society countrywide.

"I undertook the review, modernization, and implementation of procurement procedures for all government-funded projects. Prior to that, everything was a mess, and the government was losing a lot of money through the circumvention of laid-down procedures. What I did sealed all the loopholes.

Washington went on to enumerate many initiatives he had undertaken, all of which were roaring successes.

"In conclusion, distinguished members of the interview panel, my journey as an architect was a fruitful one. There were only four outstanding court cases that were hanging in the balance before I came here. Indeed, the parties in one of those cases may have hastened my departure from Earth," Washington stated.

"Thank you very much, Washington. As we promised, we will now proceed to ask several questions to seek clarifications on some things," the Chief Interviewer said.

"Paul, please roll the THP for three years after Washington joined the civil service," the First Assistant Interviewer said.

Washington was stunned when he saw himself in his formative years as a young architect. He was highly ambitious but a tard full of himself. When he joined the civil service, the idea that everyone there was corrupt was firmly set in his mind, while he was an angel sent to the Ministry of Public Works on a rescue mission.

He saw corruption in every nook and cranny of the organization. Where it did not exist, he invented it. He went a step further by publicizing it in the monthly publication of the country's Architects' Association.

Because of his zealousness, he went out of his way to lend a voice to the revision of procurement procedures. Thanks to an accommodating boss who did not want to extinguish the fire of the ambitious young man, Washington pushed through the changes. And that is how the procurement modernization became a milestone that he was proud to put on his resume.

Unfortunately, because of his aloofness, Washington stepped on numerous feet, sometimes inadvertently. He also dented the image of the civil service considerably.

The procedural changes he recommended completely stifled the workflow and caused unnecessary backlogs in the implementation of critical projects.

Analysis gradually mutated into paralysis across the organization. Washington had almost single-handedly taken government bureaucracy to the stratosphere, giving birth to new innovative forms of corruption that could never be detected even with the most sophisticated microscopes.

"Was this the modernization of the procurement procedures you referred to in your presentation?" the First Assistant Interviewer asked.

"Ah!Ah! Eh! Eh! Yes. But I must admit it did not occur to me at the time that it would have such negative impacts as I have just seen," Washington responded.

"Did you consider consulting other people who had expertise in such matters? Your profession was architecture, after all!" asked the First Assistant Interviewer.

"I admit self-conceit is evident from the recording. But I was completely blind to it at the time," I feel ashamed of myself.

"The role you played in conceptualizing and developing architectural designs for the low-cost housing program is quite commendable," the Second Assistant Interviewer said.

"You made a big difference in the lives of many individuals," the Third Assistant Interviewer said.

"There was only one point where things appear to have gone slightly astray. Paul, please fast-forward to six months before the approval of the low-cost program," the Chief Interviewer said.

The THP showed Washington talking to one of the prospective contractors in a restaurant. The contractor was a highly respected businessman.

He was known for his shrewdness in business dealings. And nobody could quite understand how he ended up winning some of the government's most lucrative tenders.

To Washington's amazement, he realized for the first time that when he bumped into the businessman at the Parklands Sports Club, it was not a coincidence. The businessman's cronies had been trailing Washington and prompted the businessman at precisely the opportune moment.

According to the Civil Service Code of Conduct at the time, Washington should have declined the offer of a cup of tea. During that unfortunate meeting, Washington inadvertently revealed some crucial information about the low-cost housing program that gave the businessman an unfair advantage over other bidders when the project was put to tender.

This incident at the sports club would later come to haunt Washington. It was recorded on video by the businessman's cronies. The businessman later used the recording to blackmail Washington into revealing other essential information regarding the contract.

The holier-than-thou architect had suddenly turned into the corrupt civil servant he had greatly despised. It was an incredibly humbling experience, as evidenced by the MSS recording that Angeline played.

The bombastic Washington looked tired and distraught after the excruciating experience of watching and listening to himself engaged in corruption.

"Thank you. The interview panel will now retire briefly in the chambers to review your case. We will be back in a few minutes," the Chief Interviewer said.

"Judith, can you see anything of interest in the BCF?" the Chief Interviewer asked.

"Yes. Several entries occurred within a span of three months after Washington met the businessman. He visited the Holy Basilica and beseeched his creator for forgiveness for the transgressions he had committed and the ones that the businessman was expecting him to commit. It shows that because Washington had previously projected himself as a beacon of anti-corruption, things were evolving in a manner that forced him to commit acts that were anathema to his very being – but Washington believed he had no choice in the circumstances," Judith said.

The interview panel returned to the Interview Room.

"We have reviewed your case closely. There is one item for which we need your clarification.

"What do you have to say about your meeting with a contractor at the Parklands Sports Club?" the Chief Interviewer asked.

"It was entirely coincidental, and I regret it ever happened.

"After the meeting, I felt trapped between a rock and a hard place, with no room for maneuver.

"But I am sure the interview panel is aware that I did not benefit whatsoever in the transaction – other than saving myself from extreme vilification if my meeting with the businessman was publicized in the media.

"My enemies in the Ministry of Public Works and the construction fraternity would never have believed that I was not compromised by the businessman – granted that what actually happened was a form of compromise.

"I remained eternally remorseful for that error," Washington said.

The Chief Interviewer asked Washington to stand up.

"Given the life you led on Earth, your actions and motivations for those actions, and the practical steps you took to steer your life in different directions, we have concluded that you belong to the classification H. The angels present will guide you to Room H to await your final judgment," the Chief Interviewer said.

"Thank you," Washington said

Three angels then ushered him to Room H.

CHAPTER 7

Room 781: Businessmen

"Businessmen are the only people who can call a 10-hour workday 'short' and a two-week vacation a 'long' weekend."
— Warren Buffett

THE WORLD IS FULL OF people who refer to themselves as businessmen. They come in all shapes and forms - from the small-time vendors who sell their wares in open-air markets in different parts of the world to the high-rollers who crisscross the globe making mega-million deals. But all businessmen have one attribute in common: selling goods or services with the motive of making a profit. Because of this, interviews of individuals whose primary vocation was doing business were the most time-consuming.

The interview of a Kenyan businessman, Johnston Kamau, is an excellent representative sample of how things unfolded in the Interview Room in relation to businessmen.

Enter Johnston Kamau

The angels ushered Johnston Kamau into the Interview Room. From his disheveled hair, it was apparent he must have mutated from a hippy to a businessman. There was a certain sense of don't-care-less in his demeanor, probably a function of the rough life he led prior to his exit from Earth. He was adorned in a brown Kaunda suit and safari boots. He was also holding a golf cap, which he periodically wore and then removed. He was a little pot-bellied, perhaps attributable to regular consumption of *nyama choma* (roast meat) and beer.

"Welcome to the Interview Room, Johnston," the Chief Interviewer said.

"Thank you," Johnston responded.

"Please introduce yourself to the interview panel," the First Assistant Interviewer asked.

"I am Johnston Kamau from Dagoretti Corner in Nairobi, Kenya. I married Christina Wanjiku one year after leaving college. God blessed us with three children, two boys and one gao (meaning girl)," Johnston said.

"I was a businessman in Kenya for 30 years before coming here," Johnston added.

"Thank you, Johnston," said the Third Assistant Interviewer.

"The angels in charge of your Room must have already explained to you in detail why you are here today, right?" the Third Assistant Interviewer asked.

"Yes, " Johnston replied.

"Good. Please give us an account of your life on Earth. Please note that from time to time, during your presentation, we may play a video of certain segments of your life. We may also activate the mind-reading system to get additional insights into the motivations of your actions and non-actions. So, let's get started," the Chief Interviewer said.

"It is my pleasure to do so," said Johnston.

"My journey in life was centered on business. It all started in high school. My parents were having challenges earning enough money to pay for my school fees. So, I was forced to do odd jobs during the school holidays to bridge the gap.

"Initially, I worked as a *matatu* (popular transportation van in Kenya) tout. But that line of work was very demanding, and the earnings were meager. To make matters worse, I was competing daily against ruffians, many of whom were drug addicts and prone to violence. It was extremely dangerous.

"So, one day, while conversing with a passenger who was transporting vegetables to Marikiti Market in Nairobi, it suddenly dawned on me that there was a better way of making money.

"I borrowed some cash from my friends to buy one day's supply of vegetables. I did some basic research and learned that the best-quality vegetables came from small-scale farms in Kahuho village, about 35 kilometers from Nairobi. However, I did not have the means to source the vegetables directly from the farms, which would have been ideal because I would have bought them at low prices. So, I decided to start with the next best option – to buy the vegetables from the middlemen at Wangige Market.

"To my amazement, I discovered that there was a money-lender stationed at the market who provided one-day credit to vegetable vendors without asking for collateral. The interest rate was high but manageable, given the small sums involved.

"I vividly recall my first few transactions. I went to the market early in the morning and borrowed some money from the money lender to supplement what I had borrowed from my friends. I then bought two large bags of vegetables. I transported them to one of the markets in the densely populated estates of Nairobi. I was amazed at how quickly I was able to sell the vegetables at a profit.

"Not only that, I struck friendships with three vendors. They asked me to deliver vegetables to them every other day of the week except Sunday. It was a stroke of luck that remained written in my memory.

"I never looked back. I religiously made my deliveries, sourced using borrowed money from the good samaritan who lent money to needy people like me and who was probably unknown to anyone other than the Wangige vegetable vendors.

"The profits I made from this simple venture gave me the real taste of business. The school fees issue became a thing of the past.

"I finished high school and joined a teacher training college in western Kenya. I had saved enough money to pay for the fees. But truth be told, I was studying merely to please my parents. Otherwise, my heart was in business.

"Therefore, upon completing my teacher training, I returned to Nairobi to continue trading in vegetables.

"After two years, I decided to change from vegetables to goats. I would travel to Masailand, buy several goats, and transport them to Nairobi for sale to butcheries.

"And just as in my first venture in vegetables, I established good relationships in Masailand and in Nairobi butcheries, all of which translated into a good trading venture that gradually grew in profitability.

"Later on, I bought land in Masailand, where I grazed my own goats and sheep. The profit margins of my business sky-rocketed.

"The major transformation of my business career happened ten years later when, by sheer luck, I got an opening in the hides and skins business. This was the jewel that was awaiting my discovery during all the years I struggled in different business ventures.

"In a short five-year period, I was able to acquire three plots in the Ruaka area in Nairobi, on which I built apartment blocks that were generating a handsome income. But I must admit, it was not smooth sailing. I ran into all manner of problems with the authorities.

"Also, I ran into a big problem during the construction of a fourth apartment block that forced me to stop any further development.

"The building collapsed literally three months before completion, leading to the loss of life of three workers. It was a regrettable turn of events because even by the time I came here, the matter was still in court.

"But I realize I have not answered your question directly. So, I will give a short, summarized answer based on the context I have just laid out.

"Firstly, when I borrowed money and bought vegetables from vendors or farmers, I added value to the lives of the money lenders, the vendors, the farmers, the owners of vehicles that I used to transport the vegetables, the Nairobi market vendors to whom I sold the vegetables, and to tens of families who bought the vegetables for consumption.

"The same applies to all the people I interacted with in the value chain of the goats and sheep business, as well as those in the value chain of the hides and skins business.

"Most of all, I employed many workers during the construction of apartments at Ruaka, not to mention the accommodation I provided to more than 90 families after the completion of the construction of three apartment blocks.

"The profits from my businesses also enabled me to take good care of my family, educate my children, and help many relatives."

"Thank you, Johnston. We appreciate your detailed presentation," the Fourth Assistant Interviewer said.

"Paul, please run the THP for the launch of the construction project at Ruaka," the Chief Interviewer said.

Johnston watched with tremendous consternation how his every move was captured in 3-D and in technicolor. The years of struggles had turned him into a wheeler-dealer of unparalleled wit. He was impressed by himself.

But there were things he did that, in retrospect, were regrettable. For example, in his zeal to speed up the apartment construction projects, he had greased the palms of several individuals in the Ministry of Lands and Urban Planning, as well as in the County government. In one particular case, he had paid a substantial sum to an official to facilitate the approval of his building plans. He knew full well the designs were not compliant with the County Zoning Regulations. Still, the temptation to break the rules was enormous, considering the incremental rental income he would get. The demand for housing was almost insatiable, and he was in a hurry to exploit it to the best of his ability.

"What caused the collapse of the apartment building?" the Fourth Interviewer asked.

"I blame it on the contractor. I came to learn that he was not mixing the cement, ballast, and sand in the right proportions, especially during the construction of the beams," Johnston responded.

"Angeline, please roll the MSS for the same period," the Chief Interviewer said.

Johnston's thoughts were laid bare before him and the interview panel:

I do not know how many times I need to inform this contractor that time is of the essence. I know the architect said we must let the cement cure within 21 days before proceeding to the next phase, but these people have no idea that time is money. I will not engage in another argument with the architect. The work must continue.

Even this thing about building only three levels. To hell with him and the County inspectors. We will build up to the fifth floor. And we have to do it in a hurry before the next inspection. Will they tell me to demolish two floors? No way. I have paid that Peter fella at the County Office to give me protection.

In any case, all these busybodies from the County office have no idea what it takes to put up this kind of structure. If they had a bank manager breathing down their necks, then they would go slow on me.

It is time to call that crooked Compliance Officer from the Construction Corporation before he decides to make one of those silly unannounced site visits. I do not want any unnecessary stories about sewage lines. The fellow has no idea about the recent sharp rise in the cost of steel. Instead of giving me all these troubles, they should be thinking about how to subsidize poor businessmen like me. That is what happens in some Western countries.

"That will be enough for now, Angeline," said the Chief Interviewer.

Johnston was dumbfounded.

"I am really sorry, but I was under a lot of pressure at the time, especially from the bank manager and the tax authorities," Johnston said.

The interview panel also requested a rewind of the THP to Johnston's days in Masailand.

Johnston was embarrassed to see an incident where he purchased a herd of goats and sheep from a shopkeeper. When he bought the animals, there was no doubt in his mind that he was buying stolen property. The purchase of the animals from a shopkeeper rather than a farmer at half the market price was sufficient evidence that there was something fishy about the transaction. But he deliberately avoided asking too many questions. On the contrary, he completed the transaction in record time to ensure he transported the animals to Nairobi as quickly as possible. He made a handsome profit.

The interview panel requested Angeline to run the MSS for two minutes from when the interviewee said to himself: "After all, I have a family to feed." As it turned out, this simple sentence was loaded with guilt.

"Thank you. The interview panel will now retire briefly in the chambers to review your case. We will be back in a few minutes," the Chief Interviewer said.

"Judith, please examine the BCF and tell us whether you see anything of interest," the Chief Interviewer said.

"The only recording that exists dates to the time Johnston was hawking vegetables. He visited the local church at Dagoretti Corner regularly. He was even a member of the choir.

"The BCF shows that he confessed and sought forgiveness for sins he had not even committed. It is a little confusing, but those are the facts in the BCF.

"The other set of entries relates to the time he was transporting the herd of sheep and goats he had procured from a shopkeeper at Narok Shopping Center. There was a bulletin in the morning news announcing the theft of livestock that fit the description of the cargo he was transporting to Nairobi.

"We can see that Johnston heard that announcement while in a shop near a petrol station where the lorry transporting the animals stopped to refuel. At that point, the BCF started capturing some data that was flowing in quite rapidly. The BCF shows Johnston praying non-stop and seeking forgiveness for handling what was clearly stolen property. He prayed for journey mercies to the final destination at Dagoretti Market, where he intended to offload the cargo. He beseeched the creator to remove all the risks of being caught by policemen before reaching the final destination.

"We can also see he sought forgiveness immediately after selling the animals, shortly after uttering the words: "..family to feed," said Angeline.

"Thank you, Angeline.

"Colleagues, it is obvious that these cases are becoming more and more complex. But that is why we are here," the Chief Interviewer said.

"I would say Johnston belongs to classification H. What do you think, colleagues?" the Chief Interviewer asked.

All the assistant interviewers concurred with the Chief Interviewer.

The interview panel returned to the Interview Room. The Chief Interviewer asked Johnston to stand up.

"We have reviewed your case closely. Given the life you led on Earth, your actions and motivations for those actions, and the practical steps you took to steer your life in different directions, we have concluded that you belong to the classification H. The angels present will guide you to Room H to await your final judgment," the Chief Interviewer said.

"Thank you," Johnston responded.

Three angels then ushered Johnston to Room H.

Proceedings continued for several more months, during which the interview panel talked to many more business people. During that time, the workload for the Third Assistant Interviewer was enormous due to the large number of excuses the technical team needed to record in the GBLE.

CHAPTER 8

Room 666: Criminals and
Riff-raff

"Son, the greatest trick the Devil pulled
was convincing the world there was
only one of him."
— David Wong

A S THE INTERVIEW PANEL AND the angels took a break, some intense activity was taking place in Room 666. Five entities dressed in black had entered the room and started making arrangements to conduct fake interviews.

Statement by Lucif, the Fake Chief Interviewer

"Colleagues. Thank you for your speedy entry into the room. I really like the arrangement of the interview section.

It is a replica of the Interview Room. Congratulations, Lucif 1. You have done us proud.

"Colleagues, remember that we have very little time. We have to work extraordinarily fast to ensure we harvest as many individuals as we possibly can. That means we have to use highly advanced interview methods.

"To that end, we will call out a particular area of expertise and ask people to indicate by a show of hands whether they were proficient in that skill during their sojourn on Earth. We will then make a quick selection of candidates for interview.

"Next. We will ask the selected candidates to introduce themselves very, very quickly. When I say quickly, I mean quickly. If necessary, we may just ask them to give us their initials and their exit location.

"Next. We will then ask them to go straight into the accounting for their sojourn on Earth piece. A few sentences will be enough.

"And please, please, please! Remember that we do not want long stories. So, when you notice a candidate veering off on a tangent, please cut them off immediately.

"Are we together?" Lucif asked.

"Yes, we are, master," Responded Lucif 1, Lucif 2, Lucif 3, and Lucif 4 in unison.

"So, let's get started, fellas!" Lucif said.

Lucif's Address to Interviewees

Lucif stood in front of the improvised Interview Section in Room 666 and asked everyone in the room to pay close attention to what he was about to say.

"Dear friends," Lucif started.

"It has come to our attention that there are some angels who have been flying around telling you all manner of things about interviews.

"We know many of you are becoming restless as you await your turn to go for the so-called interview.

"Also, we know that the restlessness has been exacerbated by the boredom and coldness of this room. We have been here for less than three minutes, and we are already feeling bored and cold.

"The good news is that we are here to show you the quick and better way to a warm and better place. A place where you will not need to worry about cold temperatures.

"It will be summer forever," Lucif 1 chimed in.

"That's right," affirmed Lucif.

"So, this is what we will do. We will focus on skills categories. What do I mean?

"We will call out a skill category, and if you were well endowed with that skill during your sojourn on earth, then just raise up your hand. We will then ask you to come in front and explain to us how you excelled in that skill.

"If we see too many hands, then we will ask you to form a queue on one side of the room so that we can move systematically.

"And please, no pushing – although you will discover quite quickly that such conduct will not be well rewarded," Lucif said, turning his head to a strange-looking character, not previously visible, with hands hidden on their back, holding something that would only be revealed at the opportune moment. The character was smiling for no apparent reason but perhaps to project a demeanor of kindness – although, clearly, not succeeding.

"Now listen carefully because this is the most crucial part. When you come in front, just mention your name and your location of exit from Earth, and finally, your competence in the skill or just a brief explanation of why you believe the skill entitles you to go on the endless summer holiday that I described earlier.

"If we find we are running out of time, we will ask you to just state your initials and give us just one sentence to explain yourself.

"After you do that, we will immediately inform you whether or not you have passed the interview and then show you where to go. Is that clear?" Lucif asked.

There was some loud murmuring in the room, so Lucif could not tell whether the answer was Yes or No.

"Let's get started," Lucif said.

Lucif 1 climbed on a stool so that everyone in the room could see them.

"Debauchery," Lucif 1 shouted.

There were only a few hands that sprung up. One individual whose Earthly sojourn was in a non-English-speaking country was heard murmuring to someone next to him: "I worked in a butchery before coming here, but I cannot say I was skillful in it."

"Okay, you, you and you. Start queuing up here," Lucif 2 said, pointing to the first three people to raise their hands.

"Others, please follow these three and hurry up!" Lucif 2 said as the queue started growing.

"Okay, you go first. And remember the drill: Name, Exit location, Explanation; then you step aside. My colleague here will then let you know where to go.

"Ousmane Souleyman, Koudougou, Burkirna Faso. My father was a butcher and slaughtered many sheep and cattle. He taught me how to do it. I became an expert and sold the meat in our butchery at Ouagadougou," said Ousmane Souleyman, then stepped aside.

"You are in the wrong queue, my brother. But do not worry. You have passed the interview. Go through that door over there. The one marked H.

"Next," said Lucif 1.

"Jeffrey Epstein. New York. Made millions of dollars trafficking young girls for the rich and famous, including some of the most powerful politicians, some of whom I hear are in Room 1201. My name was on television and social media for more than ten years," Jeffrey Epstein said, stepping aside.

"You have passed the interview with flying colors. Please follow the first gentleman to the door marked H," said Lucif 1.

Lucif 1 turned to Lucis 2 and said: "Tell the team in the warm house we have a special guest who must be given special treatment."

"Next," said Lucif 1.

"King ...,.." the person started.

"King, who?

"King Charles the Second, Westminster, England...," the King started saying but was quickly interrupted by Lucif 1.

"Yes. We know you quite well. You should not be here. But no worries. Just follow those fellas over there.

"Next," said Lucif 1.

After finishing interviews for Debauchery, Lucif 2 replaced Lucif 1 on the stool to continue with the next category.

"Murder," Lucif 2 shouted.

Numerous hands shot.

"Wow!" said Lucif 2.

"Okay! This is what we will do. Instead of your full name, just say your initials, name of exit city, and explanation in one sentence. But please, form a proper queue over here.

"Okay, you. You can start," said Lucif 2.

"A S, Durban, stabbed my girlfriend with a penknife and received instant mob justice from neighbors leading to my exit," said A S.

"Good. I like the way you have done it. That is a good example for everyone else in the queue," shouted Lucif 2.

"Go to door H over there, said Lucif 2.

"Next," said Lucif 2.

"A Dada, Kampala, slaughtered thousands of my political enemies for good reasons and enjoyed it immensely, but the world did not like it," said A Dada.

"People. Please! I said only initials. Do you know the meaning of initials? Yes. Just the first letters of your names," said Lucif 2.

"Dada. Go over there - where you see a door with the initial H written on it.

"Next!" shouted Lucif 2.

"A K, Tokyo, Japan, threw somebody through a window during judo practice and accused of manslaughter, although she was a woman," said A K.

"Sorry to hear that. Manslaughter is almost the same as murder. So, you are very welcome to the warm place. Just follow Dada to door H," said Lucif 3.

"Next!" shouted Lucif 2.

"R U, Harlem, US, shot dead a shopkeeper of Seven-Eleven who refused to hand over cash," said R U.

"Go to door H over there, said Lucif 3.

"Next," said Lucif 2.

"D R, Brazzaville, Congo, left scissors in patient's intestines during operation and accused of gross negligence, but patient's relatives insisted it was murder and used same scissors on me to cause my exit from Earth," said D R.

"Very sad indeed. But we like gross negligence, too. So, follow R U to door H," said Lucif 3.

After several more interviews, it became clear to Lucif and his team that most people on the murder queue were well qualified. So, to save time, Lucif made the following announcement:

"We are delighted with the quality of candidates we have interviewed so far. They have all demonstrated the kind of skills required to go to the land of endless summer. Therefore, to save time and ensure seamless access to the warm place, we have decided to grant an exception to all those people still waiting in the queue. All of you, please proceed to the door marked H.

There was a stampede as the interviewees rushed towards the designated door. Lucif and his team of interviewers were delighted with the progress thus far.

Lucif 3 stood on a stool to call out the next skill.

"Forgery," Lucif 3 shouted.

Countless hands were up in seconds.

"Okay! Line up in front of me. Remember, the drill is the same. So, let's go,"

"A G, Canberra, Australia, Forged cheque, but it bounced. But still accused of forgery and sent to jail even if I was technically innocent," said A G.

"That was unfair. But don't worry. You are welcome to everlasting summer camp. Just follow the queue to door H.

"K K K, Birmingham, Alabama, USA, signed my wife's signature and sent to jail because cheque belonged to her employer," said KKK. He was also directed to door H, as were many others who described their prowess in forgery.

"We will now proceed to the next skill," announced Lucif 3.

"Corruption," announced Lucif 3.

Several hands shot up.

"All of you whose hands are up, please line up here. The process will be the same as before. However, because we have saved some time in the previous interviews, please feel free to state your name fully, the location of your exit from Earth, and a one-minute exposition of why you should be given a chance to go to the warm place. Are we together?" Lucif 4 asked.

"Yes," All those in the queue responded.

"Okay, let's go," Lucif 4 said.

"G O V, Paris, France, caught red-handed bribing government official in Guinea Bissau to receive privileged government tender documents for a hydroelectric dam," G O V said.

"Thank you, G O V. You will like the warm place. No need for hydroelectricity there. Please proceed to the door marked H," Lucif 4 said.

"J H, Kangundo, Kenya, demanded a 1,000 shilling bribe to forgive a driver who was over-speeding on Kangundo Road," J H said.

"Excellent start! Please proceed with speed towards Door H," said Lucif 4.

"Next," said Lucif 4.

"R B C, Vienna, Switzerland, received a bribe to cover up a money laundering scheme perpetrated by the leader of a Latin American drug cartel," said RBC

"Thank you. You may proceed to the door marked H," said Lucif 4.

At that point, word came through the grapevine that formal interviews in the Interview Room would be resuming at any time.

Lucif and the team panicked because they had not covered many of the skills they were targeting, such as mugging, burglary, and the like. But they had no choice but to halt operations immediately.

Lucif made an announcement that was intended to reassure those who were still waiting for their turn to be interviewed.

"Friends, we have to temporarily halt operations so that we can finish processing the candidates who have gone through the interview process. We will try our level best to do this work as quickly as possible so that we can return to continue with the interviews," Lucif said.

"We are fully aware of the enormous talent that exists in this room that we can tap. For example, we have still not interviewed for assault, robbery, arson, kidnapping, embezzlement, extortion, vandalism, and many others. But don't lose heart. We will be back soon.

"Meanwhile, please polish up your resumes so that we can proceed with speed when we return," Lucif added.

"Adios!" Lucif and his team said in unison and then disappeared as quickly as they had entered Room 666.

CHAPTER 9

Room 911: Doctors

"God heals and the doctor takes the fees.
— Benjamin Franklin

THE PROSPECT OF INTERVIEWING INDIVIDUALS who spent the better part of their lives interviewing patients filled the interview panel with enthusiasm. Further, the individuals would have taken the Hippocratic Oath before starting their professional careers. This meant the panel would be dealing with individuals who were generally above average in terms of ethical uprightness. But going by the experience of previous interviews, the interview panel was ready for any unexpected curve balls. The Chief Interviewer had asked his colleagues on the panel to familiarize themselves with the Hippocratic Oath for context as they listened to presentations from the interviewees.

John Mucai

The Hippocratic Oath

I swear to fulfill, to the best of my ability and judgment, this covenant:

I will respect the hard-won scientific gains of those physicians in whose steps I walk, and gladly share such knowledge as is mine with those who are to follow.

I will apply, for the benefit of the sick, all measures [that] are required, avoiding those twin traps of overtreatment and therapeutic nihilism.

I will remember that there is art to medicine as well as science, and that warmth, sympathy, and understanding may outweigh the surgeon's knife or the chemist's drug.

I will not be ashamed to say "I know not," nor will I fail to call in my colleagues when the skills of another are needed for a patient's recovery.

I will respect the privacy of my patients, for their problems are not disclosed to me that the world may know. Most especially must I tread with care in matters of life and death. If it is given to me to save a life, all thanks. But it may also be within my power to take a life; this awesome responsibility must be faced with great humbleness and awareness of my own frailty. Above all, I must not play at God.

I will remember that I do not treat a fever chart, a cancerous growth, but a sick human being, whose illness may affect the person's family and economic stability. My responsibility includes these related problems, if I am to care adequately for the sick.

I will prevent disease whenever I can, for prevention is preferable to cure.

I will remember that I remain a member of society, with special obligations to all my fellow human beings, those sound of mind and body as well as the infirm.

If I do not violate this oath, may I enjoy life and art, respected while I live and remembered with affection thereafter. May I always act so as to preserve the finest traditions of my calling and may I long experience the joy of healing those who seek my help.[1]

If all the interviewees had adhered to their Hippocratic Oath, then their respective journeys to H would be pretty smooth. But only time in the interview room would tell.

Enter Dr. Jabulani Shaka

The angels ushered Dr. Jabulani Shaka into the Interview Room. She had neat, short, black hair tied with a band at the back of her head. A super clean snow-white overcoat hid her favorite Friday's only party dress. She wore large spectacles with expensive frames that seemed superfluous, given her white and black eyes that had never experienced even a speck of dust. Eyes that betrayed her long absences from her dusty home village, if she had ever been there at all. The only item missing to complete the doctor's image was a stethoscope, which was understandable, given that she would never need it again.

It was obvious that many patients who visited her surgery probably got cured before she prescribed any medicines – in the spirit of the Hippocratic oath she took when graduating from medical school, especially the part that said: "I will remember that there is art to medicine as well as science, and that warmth, sympathy, and understanding may outweigh the surgeon's knife or the chemist's drug."

"Welcome to the Interview Room," the Chief Interviewer said.

"Thank you," Dr. Shaka responded.

"Please introduce yourself to the interview panel," the Chief Interviewer said.

"Firstly, thank you for sparing your valuable time to interview me.

"Thank you too for coming," said the Chief Interviewer.

"My name is Dr. Jabulani Shaka. I was born in the Kwazulu Natal province in South Africa at a place called Maphumuko. My parents moved to Durban when I was still an infant. I attended school there, from primary to secondary school. I finished secondary school at the top of my class and was admitted to Stellenbosch University. I graduated six years later with a Bachelor's degree in Medicine and Surgery. That was one of the most important milestones in my life.

"I was then hired by the government and posted to Johannesburg, where I worked as a general practitioner in the Casualty Department. While working there, I met Sibusiso Shaka, a dentist who would later become my husband.

"We had two children, tweens, namely Alex and Joyce. Both of them were still in primary school at the time of my exit from Earth.

"Thank you, Dr. Shaka," said the Chief Interviewer.

"We believe the angels in charge of your Room explained to you in detail why you are here today. Is that right?" the First Assistant Interviewer asked.

"Yes, they did," Dr. Shaka replied.

"Thank you. We would appreciate it if you would please give us an account of your life on Earth. Please note that from time to time, during your presentation, we may play a video of certain segments of your life. We may also activate the mind-reading system to get additional insights into the motivations of your actions and non-actions. Please proceed," the Chief Interviewer said.

"Thank you. I believe the best place to start is from the point I completed my studies and qualified as a medical doctor," said Dr. Shaka.

"That will do, thank you," said the Chief Interviewer.

"The medical profession is unique in the sense that it provides the practitioner immense opportunities to do good in society. For example, during my first year in the Johannesburg General Hospital, I handled more than 300 cases, 20% of which were critical. And I am proud that during that period, all the patients who passed through my hands recovered. There was only one unfortunate case of an 85-year-old who was brought to the hospital a little too late after he had contracted the ailment and succumbed to the illness two days after admission.

"I was still very young and inexperienced and found that unfortunate event one too many. In later years, I came to learn firsthand that managing such extreme cases was my solemn duty, irrespective of the outcome.

"After four years of working for the government, my husband and I decided to set up a private practice. I must admit we had not done our feasibility study carefully because our clinic at Rosebank ran into financial difficulties after six months. We exhausted our savings trying to save the clinic. We later turned to a bank in Johannesburg for short-term financing, and that turned out to be the biggest error of our careers.

"My husband was forced to dabble in the real estate business while practicing dentistry. This helped to keep the bank at bay and to pay school fees.

"By sheer luck, through his real estate business, my husband found really cheap premises near a mall. And when we moved there, things started picking up very nicely. The only problem was that it was also close to some of the unsavory places in Alexandra.

"So, although the money was good, we were sometimes forced to deal with very traumatizing cases caused by acts of crime. But we held on since we had taken the Hippocratic Oath to serve mankind without discrimination. Indeed, the medical services I rendered to the residents of the Alexandra area were the most significant legacy of my sojourn on Earth before my sudden exit after an altercation with a patient over a long, outstanding medical bill.

"Thank you, Dr. Shaka. We will now ask you some follow-up questions.

"Paul here will run the video for the short duration when the 85-year-old turned up at the hospital in Johannesburg to the time of the old man's Earth exit.

Dr. Shaka was immensely surprised when a portion of her life was projected on the Hologram Platform. This was a common reaction when interviewees reached this stage of the interview process.

On the day the patient arrived at the hospital, there was nobody in the Triage section. Dr. Shaka (Dr. Jabulani Siyambiso at the time), who was the doctor on duty in the Casualty section, was in the Dentistry Department assisting Dr. Shaka for no apparent reason.

A nurse turned up 30 minutes later. She did a preliminary examination of the patient and noticed that the case required the immediate attention of a doctor. She phoned Dr. Shaka several times, but the doctor responded rudely each time. She said she was busy assisting Dr. Shaka and would see the patient within a short while. The short while stretched to 20 minutes.

By the time she returned to the Casualty department, the patient had already fainted. She berated the nurse, who had by then been joined by two other nurses, for not having taken the patient directly to the Emergency section.

The whole matter was handled very shabbily, partly because the nurses were already angry because of Dr. Shaka's disrespectful conduct in front of other patients.

That was not all. After examining the patient, Dr. Shaka instructed the nurses to take the patient to the High Dependency Unit for total parenteral nutrition – in other words, feeding intravenously. The patient was suffering from a simple case of hunger and had collapsed after the body started running out of nutrients.

But the saddest part to watch on the Hologram Platform was the patient's mistreatment in the High Dependency Unit. The patient was not even adequately secured on the bed.

Late at night, the patient started regaining strength. He started fidgeting, looking for something to clutch on as he was already disoriented in the unfamiliar environment. At that point, a sad situation mutated into a tragedy.

The patient accidentally fell to the floor from the raised bed, suffering a severe concussion, which he never recovered from.

When Dr. Shaka saw the events playing out on the Hologram Platform, she fell to her knees and started crying.

"I am so sorry," she said while still crying.

"The nurses never told me that that is what had happened," she said.

"Benjamin, please make a note of that in the GBLE, as Angeline rolls the MSS from the time the patient fell on the floor to the time Dr. Shaka pronounced him dead.

Dr. Shaka assumed a new persona on the MSS that could hardly reconcile with her utterances only a minute earlier.

Oh my God! How could this have happened?
This is unforgivable. It was the height of carelessness by these unqualified nurses.

I know I was a little unfair to them when I berated them in front of other patients. But, surely, they could have taken better care of the patient.

We obviously cannot let anyone else know about the true cause of death. Sure! It was a concussion, but we do not need to share excessive details about how the concussion occurred. If they ask, we will say that maybe it happened when he fainted and fell on the floor in the Casualty department. Yes! Brilliant! Nobody in their right mind will challenge that fact.

In any case, the poor old man comes from a disadvantaged background. He may not have any relative or other next of kin who can compel the hospital to conduct investigations.

If Dr. Shaka agrees to marry me, I will ask him that we get out of this place as quickly as possible. I cannot afford to continue working under a cloud of such a dark incident.

Dr. Shaka regretted having spoken words that were tantamount to lies. She had no choice but to apologize profusely. Even tears would not clean up her image.

"Paul, please roll the THP, the condensed version, for the period Dr. Shaka ran a clinic in Rosebank," the Chief Interviewer said.

After watching the Hologram for a while, one could not tell whether Dr. Shaka and her husband had changed their professions from doctors to wheeler dealers of Alexandra.

But it was evident that Dr. Shaka was the one in the driver's seat. She was the one who had insisted they rent premises in the expensive upmarket Rosebank area without any consideration for the customer pool in the surrounding area. They simply could not afford the rent, and blatant over-charging of the few patients who visited their clinic and prescribing ineffective medicines to ensure return visits by the patients did not help. The Shakas had effectively sacrificed the Hippocratic Oath at the altar of financial expedience.

Indeed, it was Dr. Shaka who insisted that her husband experiment in the real estate business while still practicing dentistry, despite his vehement opposition to making such a a sharp deviation from the career he had chosen and that he still loved. Were it not for the children, her husband would probably have made a different move altogether.

The interview panel did not want to interfere with the silence that ensued after Paul shut down the THP.

Dr. Shaka was dumbfounded. She did not utter a word from that point on.

"Thank you. The interview panel will now retire briefly in the chambers to review your case. We will be back in a few minutes," the Chief Interviewer said.

"Judith, can you see anything of interest in the BCF?" the Chief Interviewer asked.

"Yes. Dr. Shaka was a highly religious person. Her faith as a Christian seems to have gone several notches higher after the demise of the old man. She went to church every Sunday after the incident and even on weekdays when she had a moment to spare. This is another special case we have encountered where the interviewee unreservedly confessed for their misdeeds and sought forgiveness," Judith said.

"Thank you, Judith," the Chief Interviewer said.

The review session was somber. The interview panel reached a unanimous decision.

The interview panel returned to the Interview Room.

"We have reviewed your case closely. Given the life you led on Earth, your actions and motivations for those actions, and the practical steps you took to steer your life in different directions, we have concluded that you belong to the classification H. The angels present will guide you to Room H to await your final judgment," the Chief Interviewer said.

"Thank you," Dr. Shaka responded.

Three angels then ushered Dr. Shaka to Room H.

Proceedings continued for several more months, during which the interview panel talked to many more doctors.

CHAPTER 10

Room 1074: Lawyers

*"To sue, or not to sue, that is the
billable hour."*
— William Shakespeare

THE PROSPECT OF INTERVIEWING THOSE who spent a big chunk of their lives interviewing others was enough to cause anxiety within the interview panel. On the other hand, there was a possibility that the exercise would run more smoothly than for the other candidates. This expectation was validated after conducting the first set of 1,000 interviews. The interview of Abdi Osman was not expected to be any different.

Enter Abdi Osman

One could tell from a thousand miles away that Abdi Osman was a lawyer. The angels needed to handle him with care because he knew all his rights.

However, the new area he was to find himself in was exceptional and operated according to a different set of rules from what he was used to during his sojourn on Earth.

Before sitting down in the designated seat, he briefly removed his spectacles. He placed them in a black spectacles case. He then put the case into the inside pocket of his immaculate black jacket. His shoes were shiny dark black and could have easily reflected light to the ceiling of the Interview Room. To conclude the entry and seating show, Abdi Osman cleared his throat for everyone to hear and to be ready for his extraordinary oratory at the appropriate time in the sacred chamber of the interviewers who would determine his destiny in the afterlife.

But no! There was one final detail. Osman needed a pen and a writing pad to write his notes. The angels declined the request, which put him a little off guard.

"You will not need to take any notes. Everything you did, said, or thought while on Earth is on record and can be retrieved at any time during these proceedings at your request. The same applies to everything that will be happening in this sacred chamber," one of the angels told him.

"Welcome to the Interview Room," the Chief Interviewer said.

"Thank you," Abdi responded.

"Please introduce yourself to the interview panel," the First Assistant Interviewer asked.

"My name is Abdi Osman, Esquire, LLB., LLM, Advocate of the High Court of Kenya. I am a Kenyan by birth and was a partner in the firm of Osman and Osman before I miraculously found myself in this place. I hope as we go along, I will gain more insights from the honorable interview panel as to the precise legal justification for my being here.

"I am a father of three beautiful girls who are studying law at Oxford. They intend to join the family firm of Osman and Osman upon their respective graduations," Abdi said.

"My *alma mater* is Cambridge University in the United Kingdom. I also have multiple diplomas from Ivy League universities in the United States of America, Abdi said.

"Thank you, Abdi," said the Chief Interviewer.

"We take it that the angels in charge of your Room must have already explained to you in detail why you are here today, right?" the Chief Interviewer asked.

"Yes, but I will require a few clarifications as we go along," said Abdi.

"Yes. Please feel free to ask any clarifying questions as we go along,"

"Thank you," Abdi said.

"We will now proceed with the interview. Please give us an account of your life on Earth. Please note that from time to time, during your presentation, we may play a video of certain segments of your life. We may also activate the mind-reading system to get additional insights into the motivations of your actions and non-actions. So, let's get started," the Chief Interviewer said.

"Before I begin my presentation, can you please explain your *locus standi* for interviewing me?" Abdi said.

"Absolutely," said the Chief Interviewer.

"As you will recall from your days on Earth, it was said repeatedly in altars across the land that all of humanity was on a journey on Earth and that after their sojourn there, they would ultimately have to give an account of their life history on Earth.

"We have been mandated from up on high to interview all mankind, individually, and classify them into two categories, namely, H or H, as a preparatory step before judgment day.

"We have been directed to use methods and mechanisms that humankind can easily relate to. That is why you see the court-like setup in this room, which you are obviously very familiar with.

"The exception is that, unlike a court on Earth, the focus here is on personal accountability. In other words, every interviewee needs to represent themselves. The interview is a personal accountability session with no need for counsel to represent the interviewee. I hope that is clear," said the Chief Interviewer.

"Thank you," said Abdi.

"Well, as I indicated earlier, I am a lawyer by profession, specializing in criminal law. Having said that, my firm covered the whole gamut of legal services in order to provide a service to all citizens regardless of their individual needs.

"Therefore, even if I specialized in criminal law, I dabbled in multiple other areas when my experience and knowledge were needed.

"The mission of my firm was to secure timely and equitable dispensation of justice for criminals and victims of crime. I am proud that my firm continued to remain true to that mission, as evidenced by the numerous citations of cases by judges of cases that my firm handled.

"Examples include the celebrated case of Kanini Nduku versus the Republic, where Kanini had been wrongly sentenced to death for the murder of her boyfriend. The case became famous because the hangman fell ill on the day before Kanini was scheduled to be hanged.

"Also, on the new date Kamiti Prison had set for Kanini's hanging, an eyewitness to the murder filed a report with the police incriminating another person. One of our clients at Kamiti Prison informed us about it. We acted swiftly and obtained Kanini's release from prison within a record two weeks. The case was all over the media, giving tremendous publicity to my firm.

"This single case triggered an avalanche of criminals and victims to our firm. I was forced to hire five more lawyers to assist me in handling the cases.

"I am not supposed to say this, but I will say it anyway. The Kanini case was the trigger of my financial break in the legal profession. I will always be grateful to Kanini.

"You know, people talked endlessly about the laws of supply and demand, especially journalists who wanted to explain away incomprehensible phenomena in the economy. But truth be told, such discussions were theoretical.

"I am not an economist, but I can tell you that were it not for this Kanini case, the legal fees I charged my clients would have remained in the doldrums for ages. So, I truly owe a lot to Kanini.

"But I digress. Apart from my enormous contributions to criminal jurisprudence, I actively participated in running the Society of Lawyers of Kenya. I know there were times when the association was synonymous with acrimony. Were it not for my interventions, that label would have stuck forever.

"I am also proud of the many philanthropic activities I engaged in, especially in my home village. Many of my relatives constantly asked me to seek political office, perhaps as a Governor, Senator, or MP. But I always resisted because of the pressure of work. But I would have considered it if I had stayed on Earth a little longer.

"This brings me to a question that has been lingering in my mind since the angel in charge of our Room talked to us about these interviews. Does the concept of an "appeal" exist in this place?"

"No. Sorry. There are no appeals. The process is straightforward. You give an account of what you did when you were on Earth, and we make a determination of which classification you belong to for purposes of the final judgment on Judgment Day. And we highly doubt appeals will be allowed on that day."

"Thank you. I have nothing more to say at this time unless you would like me to clarify or elaborate on anything I mentioned during my presentation."

"Thank you."

"And you are right. We do have a number of questions," said the Chief Interviewer.

"Paul, please run the condensed version of the THP for the period Abdi handled the Kanini case," the Chief Interviewer said.

The events leading up to the case and the eventual release of Kanini were somewhat puzzling. The so-called client of Abdi at Kamiti Prison was a relative of Abdi Osman. Strangely enough, he was also on the payroll of Osman and Osman. Abdi met him from time to time to discuss anything that could have emerged in the prison that would trigger a court case that the Osman firm could potentially handle. It was essentially an ambulance-chasing operation of sorts.

Indeed, it emerged that ambulance chasing involving road accident victims was Osman & Osman's main line of business.

Further, the wealth Abdi had amassed over time was related to insurance claims paid by insurance companies that Osman & Osman failed to relay to the accident victims or their families. Any monies channeled to the accident victims, if any, were a small percentage of the court award.

"During your presentation, you told us that the wealth you accumulated was mainly from the increased level of services people demanded from you after the Kanini case.

"However, it seems that most of your money came from ambulance chasing. Which is which?" the First Assistant Interviewer asked.

"Well! You could be right. But the fact is that whether the money came from ambulance chasing, I earned it legitimately," said Abdi. The cockiness was not lost on the interview panel.

"Fair enough! Please show us two scenes of the altercations that occurred in Abdi's office when accident claim victims came to collect their insurance claim payments," said the Chief Interviewer.

Abdi could be seen berating one of his assistants for letting the claimant come to his office. He reminded the assistant that they should always tell the claimants that Abdi was in court and would not be available for several more days. In a second scene, Abdi could be seen arguing with a client who had seen him walk into his office and refused to go away until he spoke to Abdi. The display of Abdi's callousness was exceptionally embarrassing.

"I am sorry! I misled you on that one. But on the whole, I tried my best to do the best for my clients," Abdi said.

"Thank you. The interview panel will now retire briefly in the chambers to review your case. We will be back in a few minutes," the Chief Interviewer said.

"Judith, what is in the BCF?" the Chief Interviewer asked.

"It is completely blank," Judith responded.

"Colleagues, I believe the classification of this candidate is quite straightforward," the Chief Interviewer said.

"Agreed," the other interviewers said almost in unison.

The interview panel returned to the Interview Room.

The Chief Interviewer asked Abdi to stand up.

"Given the life you led on Earth, your actions and motivations for those actions, and the practical steps you took to steer your life in different directions, we have concluded that you belong to the classification H. The angels present will guide you to Room H to await your final judgment," the Chief Interviewer said.

"Thank you. It was nice meeting you," Abdi said.

Three angels then ushered him to Room H.

CHAPTER 11

Room 1201: Politicians

"Politicians are the only people who can be sworn in on a Bible and then proceed to act like they've never read it."
—Barak Obama

THE INTERVIEW OF POLITICIANS WAS a phase that the interview panel had been waiting for for a long time. They looked forward to meeting the man with a mustache and others like him. One thing was for sure. The interviews would be extended. Interviewees in Room 1201 were clearly a problematic lot, and the interview panel would have to be well-prepared to handle them. The panel decided to first dispense with the man with a mustache so that he could be separated from the other political interviewees to completely eliminate the risk of major problems in Room 1201.

John Mucai

During preparations for the interview of the mustache man, the Chief Interviewer asked Paul to run the THP for the time in 1924 when the man was on trial for a failed attempt to overthrow a government.

Statement by Mustache Man in 1924

The army which we have formed grows from day to day; it grows more rapidly from hour to hour. Even now I have the proud hope that one day the hour will come when these untrained [wild] bands will grow to battalions, the battalions to regiments and the regiments to divisions, when the old cockade will be raised from the mire, when the old banners will once again wave before us: and the reconciliation will come in that eternal last Court of Judgment, the Court of God, before which we are ready to take our stand. Then from our bones, from our graves, will sound the voice of that tribunal which alone has the right to sit in judgment upon us. For, gentlemen, it is not you who pronounce judgment upon us, it is the external Court of History which will make its pronouncement upon the charge which is brought against us. The verdict that you will pass I know. But that Court will not ask of us, 'Did you commit high treason or did you not?' That Court will judge us as Germans who wanted the best for their people and their fatherland, who wished to fight and to die. You may pronounce us guilty a thousand times, but the Goddess who presides over the Eternal Court of History will, with a smile, tear [into] pieces the charge of the Public Prosecutor and the verdict of this court. For she acquits us.[2]

The interview panel was astounded by the statement, especially the part where the mustache man spoke about Judgment Day.

It was also not lost on the interview panel that the place where the main events of the attempted coup occurred was a large beer hall.

"What on Earth was happening in beer halls in the 1920s?" the Chief Interviewer asked in exasperation at the end of the THP presentation on the Hologram Platform of Life Histories.

Enter Mustache Man (MM)

The angels ushered the mustache man into the Interview Room. During his last days on Earth, people said he was larger than life. His reputation had not preceded him in these divine quarters because he seemed a pretty diminutive figure seated in front of the interview panel.

"Is he really the man who created so much havoc and mayhem on Earth?" the Chief Interviewer asked other members of the interview panel, rhetorically and in a whisper, without expecting an answer.

He wore an angry face, which was his trademark look while on Earth. It was apparent the last time he smiled was probably in 1913, shortly before he volunteered to join the army to participate in World War I.

The toothbrush mustache completed the image that would remain ubiquitous on Earth for several decades, even after his exit. The secret behind his peculiar toothbrush mustache was to conceal his weak upper lip.[3]

The mustache man was dressed to kill – almost in the literal sense, considering his main preoccupation during his sojourn as an inhabitant of Earth.

He wore a smart military suit adorned with various military insignia. He had a shiny black belt that fitted him nicely above his waistline. It looked a little old-fashioned, but no doubt, in vogue back in the day on Earth.

The pockets of his trousers protruded outwards. They were invented by his tailors to fulfill two purposes. Firstly and foremost, to impress Earthly mortals. Secondly, to carry guns, grenades, and/or other small incendiary devices that he may have needed in cases of emergency.

The outfit was completed by black, tightly fitting boots, typically worn by high-ranking military personnel during his time. Why were they so tight? It was difficult to tell, but perhaps it was to ensure no external blood could sip through and mess up his hidden, expensive socks. Removing those boots at the end of the workday must have been a major assignment in itself and undoubtedly hazardous to the lungs during summer.

Here was the man who had created a stir on Earth and in Room 1201.

"Welcome to the Interview Room," the Chief Interviewer said.

"Thank you. I am extremely pleased to meet you, interviewers," MM responded.

"Please introduce yourself to the interview panel," the Chief Interviewer said.

"Yes, it will be my great pleasure to do so," MM said. His voice was sharp and harsh - a clear premonition of the type of dialogue that would ensue in the next few minutes.

"Let me state at the outset that before coming to this place, I had been the Fuhrer of Germany for twelve years. I am sure you all know what that means.

"Now, I would like to go back many years earlier, from my place of birth.

"I was born in Austria-Hungary at a place called *Braunau am Inn*. This is a fact that surprises many people. I moved to Germany later in my life. That is where I spent most of my life and where I started my career in politics.

"When I was young, I wanted to become an artist, but I faced all manner of setbacks in Vienna. But perhaps the setbacks on that path were blessings in disguise. There is no question in my mind that I would not have made as significant a contribution to mankind as an artist as I did in my career in politics.

"I believe it was something to do with destiny. In other words, it was an anointing that only happens to a few people in any epoch of human history," MM said.

"Thank you," said the Chief Interviewer.

"The angels in charge of your Room must have already explained to you in detail why you are here today, right?" the Third Assistant Interviewer asked.

"Yes. I am fully aware of it," MM replied.

"Good. Please give us an account of your life on Earth. Please note that from time to time, during your presentation, we may play a video of certain segments of your life. We may also activate the mind-reading system to get additional insights into the motivations of your actions and non-actions. So, let's get started," the Chief Interviewer said.

"I would be happy to do so," MM responded.

"As I told you earlier, I was really an artist when I was a young man, but society conspired to block the realization of my artistic dreams. Can you imagine even an art school in Vienna not accepting me to acquire formal credentials in art? It was so disappointing. Insulting too. But life was generous to me.

"After unsuccessfully vending some of my artworks in Munich, I volunteered to join the army to defend my newly adopted country, Germany, during World War I. I was fearless and risked my life on the front lines. My courage and diligence earned me promotions and various medals of honor, including the Iron Cross, First Class, the Iron Cross, Second Class, and the Wound Badge in Black, just to name a few.

"Frankly, if I had died during the war, and I was ready to do so, I would have fulfilled my purpose on Earth. But clearly, God had another assignment for me. He had anointed me to free the German people from the misery that Western countries had imposed on them.

"Everything happened so quickly. A non-German person had triggered the war, but some weak German leaders at the time foolishly surrendered, even without suffering defeat on the battlefield. To make matters worse, they signed the so-called Treaty of Versailles, in which they took responsibility for the occurrence of the war and agreed to pay humongous reparations to the Western countries. This was an immensely unfair, hugely embarrassing, and exceptionally humiliating situation for my German people. They effectively became slaves to their new Western masters. I could not stomach it. I had to do something about it.

"I am happy to say that one of my significant accomplishments on Earth was to free Germans from these shackles of Western domination. But I must state right away that it was not easy. It was an eleven-year journey full of ups and downs.

"I came here before I had fulfilled my mission," MM said.

"Thank you for sharing that information with us," the Chief Interviewer said.

"But please continue. We want to hear your full account until the time of your exit from Earth," the Chief Interviewer said.

"It will be a long account. Would you like me to narrate everything," MM asked. It was apparent there were some things he would rather not have talked about.

"Yes, please. We are keen to listen to your whole account. You may choose to focus on the highlights if you find it more convenient to do so.

"OK! In that case, what I will do is to focus on the context so that you can better appreciate how things unfolded," MM said.

"That is fine. But please remember our interest is to hear about your actions and motivations. If there were others involved, don't worry about them. They will give us their accounts when they come for their respective interviews. For now, just zero in on yourself," the Chief Interviewer said.

"OK! Well, as I said earlier, through the foolishness of the leaders of Germany at the time, the German people had found themselves in an almost impossible situation. So, to free them from this situation, I had to do my level best to remove these weak and cowardly leaders.

"To that end, I chose a time when they would all be gathered together so that I could wrestle the leadership from them in one fell swoop. You see, they used to visit this large bar in Munich to meet with their staunch followers.

"I asked a few of my friends to join me. We stormed the bar like cowboys in the Wild West. I fired a shot in the air to scare them and told them categorically that we were taking over the government. But things did not work as smoothly as I expected.

"The following morning, I asked members of my political party to march to the seat of government in the city center.

"If I could digress a little, I gained inspiration to use this tactic from Benito Mussolini, in Italy, who had removed an incompetent government from power simply by mobilizing his followers in the Fascist Party to march to the seat of government in Rome.

Unfortunately, the local police mobilized a large contingent of police officers who roughed us up and stopped the march.

"The police arrested me and put me behind bars for a few days.

"I was later charged with treason. My trial was perhaps the best thing that happened to my political career. It was a good stage for me to shine in full view of all the people of Germany. In fact, at that time, things were so bad in Germany, and people could see that I was their savior.

"There was no question that the judges who presided over my case were sympathetic to my cause. This became evident from the sentence they handed down after the trial. Treason was a severe offense, but I was only handed a five-year prison sentence. Interestingly, I only served nine months.

"Once again, as fate would have it, my incarceration in prison was a blessing in disguise. It was a time for introspection and to clarify my political thinking. I spent my time there documenting my political philosophy in a 600-page book. The original title of that book captured the essence of what I described to you earlier. The title was "Four and a Half Years (of Struggle) Against Lies, Stupidity and Cowardice." However, the publisher advised me to shorten the title for marketing purposes. I agreed. I published the book under the title "Mein Kampf" which means "My Struggles.

"Mein Kampf later became the manifesto of my political party. It served me exceptionally well, especially in communicating my political ideology to the German people.

"Let me also state that the imprisonment solidified my resolve to change the political system in Germany. And I did it quite successfully.

"Through some sophisticated maneuvering over four years, I rose from a mere party spokesman to the leader of the National Socialist German Workers' Party, also known as the Nazi Party, and ultimately became the Chancellor of the German Republic.

"When I became Chancellor, my first and very urgent obligation was to free Germany from the servitude to Western countries. All German people were on my side.

"In pursuance of that purpose, I initiated war against all our enemies in Western Europe and defeated them. And by doing so, I restored the dignity of the German people.

"I revived the German economy, and the German people started prospering after years of poverty and servitude.

"Unfortunately, our enemies did not just vanish. Circumstances dictated that I take a more proactive approach to protect the German people from the possibility of future attacks by our enemies – both internal and external. I spent a lot of time in the Bavarian Alps, near Salzburg, meditating about these issues.

"During the First World War, I had realized that our country was considerably weakened by enemies from within. I had considered it my mission to ensure that one day, I would deal with this issue decisively. Therefore, the opportunity uniquely presented itself when I became the Chancellor.

"I will not spend time on this subject. Suffice it to say that I put together a team that helped me deal with this matter ruthlessly and decisively.

"After some time, I also started sensing that Russia was conspiring with Western countries to attack my country. I had no choice but to launch a pre-emptive strike.

"Unfortunately, things did not go as I had expected. The war became a major conflagration that resulted in the deaths of many people – on and off the battlefield.

"I would prefer not to talk about the details of what happened. I would have wished that things had gone better, but war is always unpredictable. That will be all for now.

"Thank you," the Chief Interviewer said.

"We will now ask you a few questions to gain more insights on some of the things you have told us and others that you may have omitted," the Chief Interviewer said.

"Paul, please run the condensed version of the THP for the period MM was an artist," said the Chief Interviewer.

MM was taken aback by what he saw on the Hologram Platform of Life Histories. During his presentation to the interview panel, he had created an impression about his art skills and the roadblocks placed in his way in a manner that seemed significantly at odds with what the panel was seeing.

John Mucai

When Hitler Tried (and Failed) to Be an Artist

In early 1908, after the death of his mother, 18-year-old Adolf Hitler left his provincial hometown of Linz and moved to Vienna, the glamorous capital of the Austro-Hungarian Empire. Leaving behind his late father's ambitions for him to become a civil servant, Hitler saw Vienna as the ideal place to pursue his own youthful dream—to become an artist.

Ascent, 1889-1939, what Kubizek didn't know was that before moving to Vienna, Hitler had already been rejected by the city's Academy of Fine Arts. Though he had passed the initial exam in 1907, his drawing skills were "unsatisfactory," the admissions committee decided.

In the fall of 1908, he again applied to the Academy of Fine Arts, and again they rejected him. Over much of the next year, he would move from one cheap rented room to another, even living in a homeless shelter for a time.

Then, in 1909, Hitler finally began earning money by making small oil and watercolor paintings, mostly images of buildings and other landmarks in Vienna that he [had] copied from postcards. By selling these paintings to tourists and frame-sellers, he made enough to move out of the homeless shelter and into a men's home, where he painted by day and continued studying his books at night.

Hitler continued his artwork after moving to Munich in May 1913, selling similar scenes of the city's landmarks in shops and beer gardens. Though he eventually found several loyal, well-off customers who commissioned works from him, his progress came to a grinding halt in January 1914 when the Munich police tracked him down due to his failure to register for the military draft back in Linz.[4]

"Thank you, Paul. Is there anything you would like to add, given what we have all seen?" Asked the Chief Interviewer.

"Well! All I can say is that there were a lot of Jews in Vienna at the time, and I know they despised me. Maybe that is why they did not like my artwork," MM said.

"Angeline, please run the MSS for the 10 minutes after the interviewee sold his last two paintings in Vienna.

I know this Samuel Morgenstern is a Jew even if he is my best customer. I like his money, but I hate his guts.

Karl Lueger, the mayor of Vienna himself, has been saying that all these Jews are up to no good, anyway. Why should I doubt Karl?

Samuel must definitely be cheating me. He is rich and could have given me a better price for my paintings. He is taking advantage of me because he knows it will take time before I get a good buyer. I hate him.

Paul prompted the Chief that there was an interesting detail he had skipped when he ran the THP. It related to the period when MM was 17.

The Chief Interviewer asked Paul to rewind the THP to that period. The details that emerged were rather embarrassing.

At the age of seventeen, he was turning into a layabout, neglecting his schooling, lounging about in street-corner cafes, and wasting a lot of his time and his mother's money in writing indifferent poetry and painting atrociously bad pictures. Even his erstwhile foppishness was neglected.

He dressed carelessly, was not too particular about washing, and developed some rather unpleasant habits that one would only have expected to find amongst the coarse Carinthian peasantry from which his mother's forebears had sprung. He was, in fact, once fined five kronen for persistently urinating in public over one of the Danube bridges.[5]

MM hated himself for talking too much. The interview panel seemed to know everything. So, why bother him with the interview in the first place, he wondered. All they needed to do was to run their recordings and get all the information about him they needed.

"We know what you are thinking," the Chief Interviewer said before MM had even finished processing his thoughts.

"We will be assigning a specific classification to you. And we cannot do this without hearing an account of yourself from your own mouth. One of our operating principles is transparency so that you can fully appreciate your classification when we hand it down at the end of the interview," the Chief Interviewer said.

"Now, we will turn to a few episodes of your life that you did not elaborate on in detail," said the First Interviewer.

"Please tell us more about the confrontation with the police when you asked members of your party to march to the city center," the Chief Interviewer asked.

"Sure! The confrontation was a bit rough. The police were quite brutal. They killed 16 of our members," MM responded.

"Was that all?" the Chief Interviewer asked.

"No. There were two other deaths. Four police officers and one ordinary citizen," MM responded.

"Did it bother you that a total of 21 people had died as a result of your actions?" the Chief Interviewer asked.

"Well! You see, we were starting a revolution, and sometimes people die during such events," MM responded.

Angeline, please roll the MSS for that specific time.

I am happy that my followers are so brave.

Life is so predictable. The police have mobilized just as I was expecting. They just need to shed a little blood to turn this into a real revolution.

I know they will not harm me for fear of angering members of my party across the country and risking chaos across the entire nation.

The shooting has started. I am a genius. Now, there is no going back. I will continue pushing harder and harder and create absolute mayhem.

"Thank you, Angeline," said the Chief Interviewer.

MM was a little embarrassed by the uncovering of his real motives when he instigated the march to the city center of Munich.

"Do you have an idea of how many people died in the wars that you instigated after becoming the Chancellor of Germany?" asked the First Assistant Interviewer.

"Before I give you an estimate, I would like to state that the very nature of war is death and destruction. I would have wished that many people did not die. But to achieve victory, my army had to act very forcefully," said MM.

"We are keen to get from you even a rough estimate of the number of people who died. Was it 100, 1,000, 1,000,000 million or more," said the First Assistant Interviewer.

"By the time of exit from Earth, I think it was a couple of millions," said MM, almost shuddering at the mere mention of the word million.

"We will refresh your memory a little. Paul, please roll the condensed version of the THP for World War II," said the Chief Interviewer.

The Holgram Platform of Life Histories showed MM in meetings with his military generals, leading up to his instructions for an attack on Poland on 1 September 1939, triggering a war involving multiple nations with horrendous casualties of army personnel and civilians. As if that was not bad enough, MM was seen scheming and eventually triggering the attack of one of his country's previous allies, the Soviet Union, in June 1941. This second attack spiraled into a worldwide conflagration. The total number of deaths from these wars was around 15 million military personnel and 38 million civilians.[6]

"What do you think of all these deaths?" the Chief Interviewer asked.

"I know you have a record of my thoughts when all this was happening. Unfortunately, I was driven by greed and self-aggrandizement. With hindsight, it was not worth it, considering the misery I visited on my fellow human beings. I was chasing elusive dreams because even if I had conquered my adversaries, I would still have exited Earth at some point in time. I feel bad about the magnitude of the harm I caused mankind. I leave it to the interview panel to make of it what it chooses," MM said.

"Thank you. The interview panel will now retire briefly in the chambers to review your case. We will be back in a few minutes," the Chief Interviewer said.

"Judith, please examine the BCF and tell us whether you see any valuable information," the Chief Interviewer said.

"The BCF is virtually blank. However, there is some peripheral information the interview panel may find of interest," Judith said.

"Please go ahead - not that it will make much of a difference to our decision given what we have heard from this candidate," said the Chief Interviewer.

"The BCF indicates that the individual hardly had any religious beliefs. The only coherent record dates to when he was about seven.

He attended church at a place called Whisuntide at the insistence of his mother, who had embraced Christianity quite strongly at that time.

The interviewee was confirmed and received special lessons in divinity from the church priest.

His mother wanted the interviewee to become a priest. Indeed, he even joined the church choir and played the role of altar boy for some time. The BCF shows that during that time, he prayed regularly, in the morning and evening, and went to church every Saturday to confess his sins. He also attended Mass on Sundays. However, in the spring of 1899, his constant misbehavior resulted in the termination of his church duties. The interviewee's mother's dreams for her son to become a priest were shuttered.[7]

Later in his life, in the few instances he made references to religion, it was with the express intention of manipulating the God-fearing masses for his personal gain.

The database shows he had an almost religious zeal to do whatever it took to get rid of what he perceived as the materialistic Jewish race and, more importantly to him, to purify German society into a homogeneous Aryan race – whether the quest to achieve these purposes resulted in the deaths of people was of little concern to him," Judith said.

"Thank you, Judith," said the Chief Interviewer

"Please also ensure you have captured the relevant points for the GBLE.

"Colleagues, I believe the classification of this candidate is quite straightforward," the Chief Interviewer said.

"Agreed," the other interviewers said almost in unison.

The interview panel returned to the Interview Room.

The Chief Interviewer asked MM to stand up.

"Given the life you led on Earth, your actions and motivations for those actions, and the practical steps you took to steer your life in different directions, we have concluded that you belong to the classification H. The angels present will guide you to Room H to await your final judgment," the Chief Interviewer said.

"It was a pleasure meeting you," MM said.

Three angels then ushered him to Room H.

Man Without a Mustache (MWM)

There is a man without a mustache (MWM). He always seems immaculately dressed in a dark suit, a white shirt, and a blue tie. He has blond hair and wears an angry face, occasionally tightening his forehead, probably involuntarily, and creating several wobbly horizontal lines. He has slightly tilted lips that exacerbate his angry look. On the whole, one can tell from a thousand miles that he hails from a privileged background. As I write this book, he is engaged in the most atrocious acts in recent human history. And we are all watching him continue to do it daily.

What will this man say on the Day of Reckoning? How about the bystanders - what will they say? The author may offer a glimpse of the answers to these questions in a future volume of "The Final Accounting," depending on the action you decide to take after reading this book.

EPILOGUE

I HOPE THAT IN THE midst of all the terrible things that are happening around all of us almost on a daily basis (especially at the time of writing this book, you have found a little cheer in the preceding pages. More importantly, you have seen the futility and destructiveness of human pride, hate, racialism, braggadocio, and other similar vices that seem to afflict mankind every so often, sometimes with devastating consequences.

When all is said and done, the perpetrators of all the misdeeds eventually depart from this precious world and get forgotten.

My greatest hope, however, is that if you believe in the idea of a day of reckoning after departing from this world, you will seek to be amongst those who will be judged to be worthy of a place in the Kingdom of God.

If reading this book has made you reflect on your deeds since you miraculously appeared on this precious earth, then that by itself is the first step towards fulfilling the purpose for which we were all created.

A bigger miracle will emerge if you can take actions that will magnify the gift of life bestowed on you and others.

We saw in the different chapters of this book that simple, innocuous, but evil thoughts can lead to actions with unpleasant consequences. We also saw in the last chapter of the book that evil thoughts and subsequent actions of just one individual led to the death of millions upon millions of people. People have written hundreds of books describing and trying to explain this phenomenon. But nobody appears to have found an indisputable or palatable explanation. The tragedy is that similar events are unfolding in the world right now, on different scales, that are unfortunately resulting in untold pain and suffering for millions of people, as well as unnecessary deaths of countless helpless people.

But should we throw up our arms in despair? Clearly, the answer is "no." There are many lessons we can learn from the one true horrendous story narrated in the book and the many other fictitious ones. One big lesson is that channeling our thoughts and deeds in ways that will put us in good stead during the final day of reckoning is the right way to go. In other words – we should always think about what we will say to the interview panel in the Interview Room before Judgment Day.

BIBLIOGRAPHY

"Hitler Speech at Munich Trial 1924." Hitler speech at Munich trial. Accessed January 31, 2024. https://www.worldfuturefund.org/wffmaster/reading/hitler%20speeches/Trial/hitletrial.htm.

"NOVA | Doctors' Diaries | the Hippocratic Oath: Modern Version | PBS." n.d. Www.pbs.org. https://www.pbs.org/wgbh/nova/doctors/oath_modern.html#:~:text=I%20swear%20to%20fulfill%2C%20to.

Bunting, James. (1976) 2007. *Adolf Hitler: His Untold Story*. Mumbai: Jaico Publishing House.

Pruitt, Sarah. "When Hitler Tried (and Failed) to Be an Artist." HISTORY, August 10, 2023. https://www.history.com/news/adolf-hitler-artist-paintings-vienna.

"Defense Casualty Analysis System," n.d. https://dcas.dmdc.osd.mil/dcas/app/conflictCasualties/ww2.

NOTES

1 "NOVA | Doctors' Diaries | the Hippocratic Oath: Modern
   Version | PBS." n.d. Www.pbs.org.
   https://www.pbs.org/wgbh/nova/doctors/oath_mod
   ern.html#:~:text=I%20swear%20to%20fulfill%2C%
   20to.

2 "Hitler Speech at Munich Trial 1924." Hitler speech at
   Munich trial. Accessed January 31, 2024.
   https://www.worldfuturefund.org/wffmaster/reading/
   hitler%20speeches/Trial/hitletrial.htm.

3 Bunting, James. (1976) 2007. *Adolf Hitler: His Untold Story*.
   Mumbai: Jaico Publishing House.

4 Pruitt, Sarah. "When Hitler Tried (and Failed) to Be an
   Artist." HISTORY, August 10, 2023.
   https://www.history.com/news/adolf-hitler-artist-
   paintings-vienna.

5 Bunting, James. (1976) 2007. *Adolf Hitler: His Untold Story*.
   Mumbai: Jaico Publishing House.

6 "Defense Casualty Analysis System," n.d.
   https://dcas.dmdc.osd.mil/dcas/app/conflictCasualties
   /ww2.

---

[7] Bunting, James. (1976) 2007. *Adolf Hitler: His Untold Story.* Mumbai: Jaico Publishing House.

BOOKS BY JOHN MUCAI

Shamba Shenanigans: A Collection of Riveting True Stories

A collection of riveting true-life experiences. Some of the stories are hilarious; others are thought-provoking, while others are likely to evoke different emotions as the story unfolds. Each story has one or more useful life lessons.

The Endless Search for More: A Collection of True Stories on Money Matters

A collection of true stories that revolve around our continuous search for "more." And while this trait is essential for the long-term sustainability of humanity, John Mucai suggests that we must always strive to appropriately calibrate our desires. And more importantly, adopt a problem-solving mindset in our never-ending quest for "more."

Historical Snapshots of The Great: What Can We Learn from Them?

The quality of life that we enjoy today is a function of the many commendable actions done by individuals in different spheres of life. Some of these people came before us many years ago, while others live amongst us. This book explores the lives of some significant historical figures to find out whether they had any common attributes that we can emulate.

Seeking The Right Path: A Search for Spiritual Enlightenment

This book is a chronicle of a personal search for spiritual enlightenment. John Mucai starts by finding out what religion means. He then looks at the different religions and zeros on five major ones: Christianity, Islam, Hinduism, and Buddhism. These religions have a combined following, comprising about 80% of the world's population. He looks at their beliefs, practices, and sacred texts.

Most importantly, many complex questions emerge from the texts. While the book would be of immense interest to theologians, it is not a book on theology. Instead, it is an attempt by the author to seek spiritual enlightenment by sifting through the religious literature freely available to any ordinary citizen of the world.

The author's findings are illuminating and hopefully give believers and non-believers a new perspective on religion.

Multiple Dilemmas: A Fictional Story of Multiple Ethical Dilemmas Based on True Historical Events

Multiple Dilemmas is a thriller based on historical events that raise significant ethical questions. The book delves deeply into challenging situations where ethical considerations are paramount, but the right choices are not clearly evident. The twists and turns in the story will keep the reader entranced for several hours.

Ngurario: A Traditional Kikuyu Marriage Experience

Ngurario is a true story of the multiple steps that John and Susan went through to formalize their marriage according to Kikuyu traditions. The book delves deeply into the drama, excitement, and joy they experienced along the way, right up to the final step in the journey, namely, an elaborate and colorful ceremony called *ngurario*.

Reminiscing On Basics: Fascinating Science and Maths Ideas for Everyone

Some ideas in science and maths are so fascinating it is a shame that they are inaccessible to many people. This book is an attempt to fill the gap. Perhaps the curiosity triggered by these ideas will put a new intellectual journey into motion for some people, as it has done for the author.

One Day in The Year 3000

Nobody knows what the future holds one thousand years from now. But one can make some wild guesses. This book peeks into that distant future.

Stratagem: Developing a Strategic Mindset

Have you ever attended a strategy meeting and wondered whether everyone in the forum had a clear understanding of what strategy meant? If you have, you are not alone. Interestingly, many such meetings roll on smoothly with impressive outcomes. That phenomenon is the ninth wonder of the world. Some participants probably spent many hours after the meeting engrossed in self-doubt or guilt, depending on how loudly they spoke during the session. A cold or hot beverage usually works wonders during such moments of self-reflection.

If you are one of those who experience self-doubt but usually emerge from strategy discussions with your conscience intact, you must count your blessings. You are a brave survivor. But whatever category you belong to, you have the cure for strategy fuzziness right at your fingertips right now. Strategem describes strategy with exceptional lucidity. Well-thought-out strategies are essential not only for business success but also for success in personal life.

Archetypes of Human Existence: A New Perspective

Out of the more than seven billion people who inhabit the Earth, no two are exactly the same. Even tweens have differences. Every individual has been bestowed by nature's unique attributes. And yet, the behavior of human beings can be reduced to a few archetypes. At the heart of the matter, each human being is one single entity comprised of a mind and a physical body, a mind that yearns for happiness and a body that longs for sustenance. And it is the interplay of these two needs that creates the different archetypes of humans. This book explores a few of the archetypes. It discusses how the ideas around archetypes converge to offer a new perspective on fundamental questions that existentialists have been grappling with for ages. The people described in the second chapter of this book are entirely fictitious.

Any resemblance of their names to real people is purely coincidental. However, the characters are real and live among us. You may recognize some of them in your local community, your network of friends, or even in other human networks to which you are directly or indirectly connected.

Number One: Nothing Else Seems to Count

In the modern, highly competitive world, doing well in any competition is not enough. Being number one is what counts. This book traces the lives of five colorful individuals. They are winners in their unique ways from the early stages of their lives. We experience intimately the twists and turns that occur as they enter early adulthood and get embroiled in a contest anchored in the pursuit of business success and love. At some point, each character will realize that things can become highly complex, emotionally draining, and even dangerous when love is in the mix. The outcome of their respective pursuits to be "number one" is astounding. Indeed, the way the story ends offers readers tremendous food for thought.

Fun and Grit: Encounters of Farming Hobbyists

The stories in this book are primarily about people- the people of the shamba (small farm). After working for one of the biggest multinational companies and dabbling in a small-scale farming hobby, one of my insights is that every experience, whether pleasant or unpleasant, gives life its flavor.

Indeed, some of the unpleasant experiences add more spice to life. Having a nice laugh about something is the magic trick in many cases. Laughter is undoubtedly the best medicine for the soul.

INDEX